'HOW'S YOUR DAD?'

'HOW'S YOUR DAD?'

MICK CHANNON JNR

RACING POST

First published in Great Britain in 2016 by
Racing Post Books
27 Kingfisher Court, Hambridge Road, Newbury, Berkshire, RG14 5SJ

10 9 8 7 6 5 4 3 2

ISBN 978-1-910498-94-1

Cover designed by Liz Platt
Typeset by J Schwartz & Co

Printed and bound in the UK by CPI Group (UK) Ltd, Croydon, CR0 4YY

www.racingpost.com/shop

CONTENTS

DEDICATION TO ALAN BALL

Dear Alan,

Well, here it is. I know it's not what you told me to do, but it's the next best thing. I'd love you to be here to read it.

When we were sitting together, just you and I in Australia, and you told me to go and do something for *myself*, I took it all on board. It's just that standing up on the after-dinner circuit and relating second-hand tales that I've experienced alongside someone who actually *had* achieved something, would have made me feel like some sort of a fraud.

That's not doing something for *myself*.

I suppose writing it all down has been for myself, but I'm still eclipsed. I wish you were still here to laugh at me and tell me your latest crap joke. I wish you were still here full stop.

If you were, you wouldn't need to ask, because you'd know before I did.

So we'll start with the first question everyone asks me: 'How's your dad?'

He's good, mate. He's had a tough year and, if you hadn't left us when you did, you might have made him see sense and pull back and enjoy life a bit more, rather than continue to plunge headlong into every minute of every day. Like a lunatic.

I still doubt that would change him, though.

I still remember the times you'd tell him to wind his neck in – and he did. Apart from Phil, nobody is around to do that these days.

Phil doesn't bother any more, but I'd like to think that life has kicked the old man in the bollocks enough this time around to make him realise that nothing lasts for ever. It's been a tough year for him but he remains the same as ever. You'd be proud of him although he never stops to appreciate what's around him. Nor does he consider the facts.

He's had a yellow card.

You just got a straight red.

We *all* miss you, Alan.

Anyway, you pop up from time to time in this book. Your advice, your laughter, your banter and your ability to see the best in everyone still inspires me. If you were more responsible at times, less of a footballer, you might have been more responsible with yourself. But that wouldn't have made you, you.

I know another man like that.

Neither of you listen – you can't and he won't, but I guess that's why you both had the lives you've had.

And you live on, for many of us anyway.

I hope this makes you proud.

MICHAEL

Alan Ball MBE, World Cup winner 1966, League Championship winner 1970. Born 12 May 1945, died 25 April 2007 – three months after the holiday in Australia.

With Alan at Royal Ascot 1999

ACKNOWLEDGEMENTS

I feel the need to justify why I've written this. In the spring of 2014 my friend and golfing nemesis John Marston went in for an operation to remove a growth from his bile duct. He never came out.

That got me thinking. Quite a lot, actually. I started thinking about everything: myself, obviously, but also all of the chaos around us that none of us have any control over, even when we think we do.

It's how to accentuate the positives that really matters.

It's not always easy, of course, but Marsie's death made me try to make some sense of it all.

I didn't know how to, so I started writing it down. I wasn't chasing the meaning of life but I did want to understand what I felt right there and then.

So I emailed a tribute to Marsie that was published in the *West Ilsley Newsletter* in May 2014. I also posted it onto my Facebook page.

I was touched by the response both from people who knew John Marston and from those who could empathise with what I'd put down. The irony of this process was that I realised what I'd written was totally devoid of ego, yet people seemed to like something *I'd* done. It helped me to understand what had just happened: I'd managed to put what Marsie meant to me in a box through writing about him. Which was ironic under the circumstances. Marsie was the first truly close personal friend that I'd had die on me. The bastard.

I then wrote about my memories of a car crash that my father and brother were involved in back in August 2008. My dad's friend was killed in that accident, which followed on the back of losing Peter Osgood and Bally in the preceding two years. Remembering my dad in hospital after the car crash while he was trying to come to terms with the death of yet another close friend brought Marsie's demise into even sharper perspective. I realised that it doesn't matter how good life has been to you, or the privileges some of us are fortunate enough to enjoy, things can still get pretty ugly.

So I wrote about the car crash and showed that to my friends as well.

They started telling me to send it to someone. *Anyone.*

It took some courage and plenty of time but I eventually sent Marsie's tribute and my account of the car crash to the journalist I admired above all others in horseracing. I sent it to Alan Lee of *The Times.*

I was walking from the grandstand at Uttoxeter Racecourse on 31 October 2014 when Alan Lee appeared beside me.

'I've read it,' was all he said.

I had immense respect for him as a writer. 'I thought I'd put you in an embarrassing position!' was all I could come up with in response.

'It's raw. *Very* raw – but it's also honest. Keep writing it down and keep sending it to me. I'll be in touch, because I think we should meet for a proper chat.'

We were by the winners' enclosure. Sgt Reckless had just returned after taking a beginners' chase, and I watched Alan walk over to get some quotes on the winner from Henrietta Knight.

Things progressed from there. When I finally met Alan Lee again he had a plan. It was February 2015: 'I know you're worried about what to do with all this stuff so I suggest that you do a diary of the racing season and try to fit all of the other writing you've sent me in around it.' We were in the Crown & Horns in East Ilsley, separated by a pot of tea and a pint of Guinness. He added milk to his cup before continuing: 'Start with the Cheltenham Festival and finish it at the end of the Flat season in November. It's worth writing down as you go along because some of it is very strong. I'm intrigued by your friend Marsic. It's raw, like I say, but I do like it. If nothing else, you've made *me* smile.'

So that's what I did. Luckily, Alan Lee shared it with journalist, author and broadcaster Brough Scott, and he continued the encouragement and saw through what Alan had begun: '*Keep writing.*'

I'll be honest; at times I wanted to stop. At times I felt that not only was I betraying my dad in doing this, but also that he might never forgive me for being so honest.

And not only that. Halfway through the year I realised that this wasn't just a diary of a year on the road, mainly losing but occasionally winning with racehorses. I realised that it was an account of my relationship with my dad. It moved entirely away from sport or my life working *with* my dad. It became a time when I was forced to consider working *without* my dad. As I say, this wasn't what I'd planned for at all.

'Make sure you're doing this for the right reason. If you're doing it for attention, it won't work because it becomes all about you. If you're doing it because it helps you then that's good enough – but be honest. That's the best you can be.' I'd like to thank Brough Scott for that advice. I'd like to thank him for understanding.

I'd also like to thank Alan Lee for taking an interest in an email I sent one Sunday afternoon in September 2014. His reaction was warm, considerate and remarkably generous. Alan's input, as with John Marston's and Alan Ball's earlier influences on me, cannot be underestimated.

Alan Lee died in December 2015 at only 61 years of age. I didn't know him well, but I liked him immensely and respected him even more. He was the same age as Bally.

Life *is* funny, though. I'd hate you to think that this is a maudlin tale of doom, death and depression. Of course, I've thought long and hard about the fallout from this book and I've worried about how people would judge me. I'm also well aware that having now entered my forties, accusations of this being the classic symptom of a mid-life crisis will abound. I'd also be a fool to rule that out entirely.

There is hope and there is optimism to follow though, and you'll hopefully get to that in the following pages, but not before we begin with an escapade that typifies my life. As Alan Lee said, 'It's very raw,' and throughout this book some of the language is atrocious. You have been warned.

So we'll go back to my university days to kick off with. They were great days that I was determined to fill with fun and very little responsibility. However, just when you're having the time of your life and you think you're flying high, all too often you fall to earth with a rather large bump.

Mick Channon Junior
April 2016

THE FALL

REDLAND ROAD, BRISTOL, FRIDAY 5 MAY, 1995

I remember getting up. Confused and disorientated but, absurdly, I was utterly aware of where I was. I was on the garden patio outside the ground floor flat. I knew there and then that things had gone a bit wrong. *Really* wrong, in fact.

I recalled flashes of the conversation I'd had with myself when I'd got home the night before. While I conceded that sleeping on the roof was not an altogether great idea, there was the valid argument that the sunburn I'd suffered on the previous afternoon would make a night's sleep indoors almost unbearable.

It was a stuffy student flat at the best of times. I had an attic bedroom with a mattress on the floor and very little else. The recent spring heatwave had taken all of us by surprise, so the decision was made: the sun lounger I'd dragged through the skylight window and onto the lead-lined roof extension the previous afternoon was the best place to be.

The majority of my numerous bad decisions in life have invariably been made in haste, under pressure or when pissed. That evening, I'd been very pissed.

A couple of hours later and I was 40 foot below and in a lot of trouble.

I'd somehow made it to the back door of the ground floor flat. I had no idea what time it was but it was still dark and I was well aware that I was stark bollock naked.

Sheer terror enveloped me. *Girls lived in that ground floor flat.* We'd been out that previous night to celebrate a twenty-first birthday. I knew the girls as neighbours, but not that well. I did know I was gargling blood. I was aware that my entire upper body was slumped off-kilter to the right, the arm all but useless and my brain almost completely scrambled but for two facts on which my focus was crystal clear. *I'd just fallen off the roof of a second floor flat, and I was stark bollock naked.*

The committee responsible for the previous night's sleeping arrangements reconvened in my head: 'Michael, you're fucked here – knock on the fucking door.'

'But there's girls in there – I've got my knob and bollocks out in the back garden.'

'Never mind that, all you can taste is blood – that's never a good sign and you can't stand up properly.'

'I don't want to knock on the door. I can't knock on the door. I'm stark bollock naked outside a flat full of female students.'

'Knock on the door or you're fucked.'

This conversation with myself seemed to go on for about five minutes, but I suspect that thirty seconds is a more accurate timescale.

I knocked.

Eventually the door opened but my recollections of what happened next are rather blurred. Screams, pandemonium and confusion were the major features of this brief but all too chaotic moment, as well as the overwhelming sense of embarrassment that still shadows me to this day. Teenage girls were running and screaming all over the place in the way that only they can when confronted at four in the morning by a bleeding, battered, bol-lock-naked housemate who lived two floors above them.

Then Pughie arrived. My mate Pughie, whom I'd been laughing with in an Italian restaurant just a few short hours earlier. The first thing I wanted was a towel. He laid me down somewhere and started asking me questions. I wasn't that lucid.

'It hurts, Pughie, it hurts, it hurts. Pughie, it hurts,' was all I could muster over and over again, although I do remember thinking, 'What the fuck is Pughie doing here?'

Pughie had done rather well for himself the night before. I recall an ambulance crew arriving, but things were getting a bit hazy by then.

Then there was a very exciting time in a hospital room. On the telly I think they call it 'Crash' where loads of medical people are shouting stuff all at once. I remember being stabbed in the chest by someone. It hurt, but it didn't hurt, if that makes any sense – it felt like a release. All I could really think at the time was, 'This is mental.'

A nice person was asking me questions. She sounded interested in me and had the sort of tone that made me feel more like a guest and less of an absolute dickhead. My guess is that it was about five or six in the morning. 'Is there anyone we can contact, Michael?'

I reeled off my mum's number and address and my dad's too. I was flying this test. I'd not lied when they'd asked me if I'd been drinking – 'about eight pints of lager, loads of wine and vodka' – and now I'd nailed the contact details of Mum back home and my Dad's at work. He was *always* at work.

There was a conversation with my dad on the phone. I can't have held the receiver, surely? I just remember the chat. I was fine: 'Daft accident, don't worry, see you tomorrow.' The sort of forthright sense of false confidence exuded by an adolescent pretending he's not pissed in front of his parents.

I remember nothing for quite some time after that. In medical terms, I was a bit worse than pissed. In layman's terms, I was fucked.

QUEEN MOTHER CHAMPION CHASE DAY

THE CHELTENHAM FESTIVAL, WEDNESDAY 11 MARCH 2015

It's a weird feeling, attending the Cheltenham Festival with runners. It's the Mecca of National Hunt racing but it used to be a social sideshow before we inherited Henrietta Knight's jump horses upon her retirement three years ago.

It was once just a jolly boys' outing, a good reason for the Flat racing lads to attend a major race meeting with little or no regard to the outcome. I used to go with the Flat jockeys based in and around Hungerford. Most of them are settled down now, many of them have kids, but we used to get properly stuck in with the usual drunken stupidity that would make us laugh, recalling the states we'd get into once the serious business of the Flat racing season began in the long summer months.

Today, though, is all about Somersby, an 11-year-old Festival favourite who has never won at the meeting but has turned up for the past seven years and performed with real credit, finishing second in last year's Champion Chase and always proving a fly in the ointment. He's a professional loser in that sense, but always the yardstick against whom the rest are measured. If they want to win, they often have to beat Somersby.

In many ways, he takes the pressure off. He's not good enough to win, but he belongs there to keep everyone else honest. If there's a chink in the opposition's armour, Somersby will find them out and he'll get a cheer from his underdog fan club along the way.

He's as talented as he is neurotic. He doesn't want a friend in the world and just does his own thing. When he first arrived from Henrietta's, we tried to train him alongside other horses. That was the first cock-up. He's not really a fan of other horses, and is even less accommodating with human beings. He's a little sour and very set in his ways, but talented individuals eventually get their own way. They can't be changed, they know they're good and act accordingly.

Speaking of such, the old man drove us there. He's a 66-year-old racehorse trainer, an arthritic workaholic and a grumpy old bastard. He always drives, he always knows best, even when the facts are stacked against him, and control is *everything*. Driving, talking, shouting, bollocking, blaming and berating – these are all traits that he displays with complete conviction and prolific frequency. He's a remarkable human being.

I'm the soakaway, the buffer. I listen and act but, occasionally, I offset the repetitive sidekick role that I fill for 99 per cent of the time.

For example, I always have the upper hand when we play Radio Two's PopMaster quiz. I hammered him on the way to Cheltenham today, a facile victory due to my ability to focus on a subject other than horseracing for more than six seconds, and an awareness of time, space and popular culture.

Road rage distracted him and that too played a key role in today's victory, although the outcome was seldom in doubt due to the fact that the only two answers I've ever heard Mick come up with on PopMaster are 'Elton John' and 'Rod Stewart', even when the question being asked requires the name of a female artist. The correct answer is often greeted by the response, 'Never fucking heard of them – how the fuck am I supposed to know that?' I haven't even got a great knowledge of music, to be honest, but I do have an awareness of the world around me.

Once we'd arrived, we battled through the crowds and avoided a tantrum at the owners' and trainers' entrance on account of the fact that I brought the correct badges, an irrelevance in Mick's mind, and made our way in. We were stopped by two or three racegoers who asked him to sign their race cards, which he does pleasantly enough, but he doesn't go overboard. 'Who the fuck wants an old fucker like me to sign their race card?' he asks as we walk on – rhetorical questions are another major part of his armoury. I seldom respond because his bemusement with the modern world is all encompassing and ever-present. He wants to train horses, run horses, go home and train them tomorrow. That's *all* he wants to do.

It was a little different twenty-four hours earlier. Every now and then you get a glimpse of the man who makes it all worthwhile. Funny, engaging, inspiring and incredibly well loved. He wouldn't have been aware of it, but for an hour or two in the company of old friends and racing professionals on the first day of the Festival he was in sparkling form.

People genuinely like him and you can see why. It's a mix of admiration and appreciation of where he's come from and what he stands for: no bullshit, no minced words and complete honesty. He's brutally uncomplicated and searingly to the point. If people don't like him, they really don't like him. If they like him, they love him. The ultimate Marmite man.

Yesterday, Sgt Reckless finished sixth in the Arkle Chase and ran well enough considering he'd only had one run over fences before in his life, at Uttoxeter. He's a horse that cannot handle soft ground, so he's basically been sitting in his box waiting for the ground to dry out this winter, and the fact that it only did so on the eve of the Cheltenham Festival meant that he was woefully inexperienced to tackle the demands of a championship race.

He's by far the best horse I've known in my seven years as Mick's assistant, beating horses of real class by lengths back home. But that has never been transferred to the racecourse, on the big stage. So we've got a National Hunt horse on our hands who can't run on soft ground, which is something of a drawback when the season runs from autumn through to the spring. When I say that he can't run in soft ground, what I mean is that he's *half* the horse he could be. He destroys horses at home on the gallops at West Ilsley, and beats Flat horses over six furlongs in the spring. I remember a horse we had called Amralah, and Sgt Reckless beat him by three lengths while carrying a stone more in weight over a mile. Amralah won a Group 1 in Australia when he left us. The Sergeant is so talented yet so flawed in the winter. 'It's no surprise to me that it always rains in the fucking winter. It has done since I was a kid and I'm no fucking genius,' is Mick's assessment of the situation.

Knock House finished fifth in the last, a great run for a young horse and, on the whole, there was plenty to take out of the day. Yesterday's time in the owners' and trainers' bar reflected that. We laughed and laughed until Mick had a craving for fish and chips and wanted to go home.

Everything in jump racing revolves around the Cheltenham Festival though, and it looked like another year was all but over. Somersby was our last runner of the week and a 33/1 outsider today. He received very little attention from the pundits and was considered to be a spent force, just making up the numbers.

Last year's Champion Chase winner Sire De Grugy and the 2013 winner Sprinter Sacre were lining up alongside Dodging Bullets, who was the last horse Somersby finished runner-up to, in a Grade 1 race in the Tingle Creek at Sandown back in November. It was a race packed with top quality contenders. Somersby left the parade ring first and went down the walkway onto the track. He's freaked out in the past when a jockey has got on him too early so, as ever, I legged up jockey Brian Hughes before the parade in front of the grandstand. By his standards, Somersby had taken everything in his stride so far. Last year I legged up A. P. McCoy on the track at the Punchestown Festival only for the horse to decide he didn't really fancy running in Ireland. The sight of the greatest jockey of all time trying to get Somersby to canter to post while the horse decided to moonwalk backwards up the walkway towards the parade ring will live long in my memory. It's been hard enough dealing with the inferiority complex I have of mixing with the great and good of jump racing, but when that happened I started to wish I was working at the golf range in Winchester, or stocking shelves in Asda in Chandler's Ford again. Even the usher's job I'd held down for three months at the bingo hall in Lordswood seemed preferable as the horse we'd put A. P. McCoy on insisted on reversing up the walkway while I waved my arms about a bit and made stupid noises. I just felt like a total dickhead (and when Somersby begrudgingly lined up he went and ran like one).

Today, though, Somersby wanted to be there. He charged down the canter towards the start and I took up a position on the rails by the final fence next to our travelling head lass Lesley White and Somersby's lad Raheem.

They jumped off for one of Cheltenham's biggest events. The Champion Chase is run over two miles and twelve fences, and

Somersby settled about six lengths off the pacesetter Special
Tiara in fourth position. He's never perfect, Somersby, and often
makes a mistake at at least one fence but, by his standards, he
travelled and jumped well throughout. Three fences from home,
he was still going well and jumping as well as Dodging Bullets
and Special Tiara with nothing else looking like a danger in
behind.

This was the Queen Mother Champion Chase and I wouldn't
have wanted to be in a better position, or travelling better than
we were.

'Lesley . . .'

'Don't say a thing, Michael!'

'Lesley . . .'

'Shut up.'

'LES-LEY . . .'

'Michael, shut up!'

They turned for the short run-in and Somersby swung quite
wide into the straight, but as soon as he straightened up he
started to charge up the hill. He jumped the second last upsides
Dodging Bullets and, with Special Tiara beginning to fall away,
I completely lost it.

'GO ON, BRIAN, GO ON, BRIAN, GO ON, BRIAN, GO
ON, BRIAN, GO ON, BRIAN!'

They jumped the last with Dodging Bullets just in front,
but Somersby again stuck his neck out and dug in to claw
back the deficit. I can't recall what happened at that point
with any certainty but I began to regain my composure as
Dodging Bullets again edged ahead and the game was clearly
up. Somersby, the old lad, battled on and went down by just
over a length, but I was beaming. It's difficult to explain if
horseracing doesn't grab you – and I often feel embarrassed

Lesley, Somersby, jockey Brian Hughes and Raheem

by my behaviour when I go to bed after acting like a top-level nutcase earlier on in the day – but it's an emotion that I find impossible to control.

The more dignified racing professionals have been known to doff their hats or turn round and kiss their other half with humility when they have a big-race winner. They'll cheer, and although sometimes they look on the brink of losing composure in an exciting finish, they seldom do. We, however, seldom win many big ones, and just being in with a chance at the end of a major race means that I always act like a total nutter. It's humiliating and possibly frowned upon, but I'm a huge advocate of the practice as, I'm happy to say, are several others in the game.

One of my mates, after seeing me deal with disappointed owners on a fruitless day at Haydock Park, described my job as,

'Introducing successful people to failure,' and it often seems that way. Owning a racehorse is expensive and they can't all be good, but if you lose perspective on the bigger picture, the shame of failure can often overwhelm you as you try in vain to emphasise the positives on what is basically a demoralising outcome.

So, the big moments have to be enjoyed, and Somersby's defeat today felt like a big moment. We'd lost, but in the most thrilling fashion, and we were completely unfancied, the archetypal plucky losers. I walked back to the winners' enclosure with Somersby through the crowds with so many compliments ringing in our ears it was quite surreal. There aren't many sports that see the beaten so openly celebrated, but this was one such an occasion. Racing can often be a vicious game – a blame game where everyone thinks they can train a racehorse better than the trainer if only they had a few spare hours in the day to do so – but today was great.

I remember hugging Somersby's owner Tim Radford who, along with his entire family, took a hell of a leap of faith in embracing Hen's suggestion that their band of eight horses should be trained out of what is primarily a Flat yard three years ago. We've never had a Cheltenham Festival winner but today was almost as good. It was heart-warming, uplifting and exhilarating.

As we drove away, Mick let out a groan and just said, 'I'm fucking gutted. We can't have a winner for Tim at Cheltenham.'

'We've had a good couple of days,' I said, trying to look at the positives. 'Things are all right, the two-year-olds are almost ready and you've got the reunion night with the lads on Friday. That'll be a good evening.'

He didn't respond, but I know he's already dreading the Friday drive to Norwich. We had to convince him to commit to it because, once he's there, he'll roll back the years and be the bloke he can be when he's at his very best.

Mick, Tim Radford and Brian Hughes

Thirty years ago Mick was a veteran footballer living out the last few years of an incredibly successful career.

Thirty years ago, my dad won the Milk Cup at Wembley with Norwich City.

THE MILK CUP FINAL

WEMBLEY STADIUM, SUNDAY 24 MARCH 1985

As a football-obsessed kid, I was *the* complete anorak. It was what I'd grown up with, all I knew and all I cared about. By 1985 I'd turned ten and I'd already memorised every FA Cup final result, the goalscorers, the captains and the managers. In many cases I can tell you the results of matches that took place decades before my conception. Indeed, my childhood stands as a testimony to an all-consuming obsession with regard to the FA Cup, a football tournament that I only really tuned out of once football became unavoidable on the telly.

Back then, only a handful of games were ever shown on the telly. Live football was like Christmas and, as a result, my memory works alongside a backdrop of FA Cup winning references: John Lennon died in 1980 (West Ham 1 Arsenal 0); the miners' strike truly boiled over in 1984 (Everton 2 Watford 0); and I lost my virginity in 1990 (Manchester United beat Crystal Palace 1–0 in a replay). What a tragic gauge against which to measure your time on this planet.

I'm not alone, though, when I say that FA Cup final day on the telly was the defining moment of the year. It had *everything*: Gerald Sinstadt and Martin Tyler in the team hotel at breakfast, Tony Gubba on the team bus and Freddie Starr joining Tarby on the hallowed turf when the teams arrived. I recall Bernie Clifton

Mum, dad, me and Nicky and the only thing that mattered

and his ostrich being there one year, and I even phoned in and got on the telly to ask for Southampton's 1976 FA Cup goal to be shown because my dad was in the studio as a pundit with Brian Moore and the Saint and Greavsie in 1984.

FA Cup final day was also the one day of the year that you could fall in love with and root for a club other than your own.

In the mid-1980s I was besotted by Everton. Although they beat Southampton in the 1984 semi-final at Highbury (I was there and I still hate Adrian Heath), they seemed to be in every Cup final that took place at that time, apart that is, from the Milk Cup final of 1985.

I can well imagine today how much of a dross match Norwich City against Sunderland would have seemed to the general public back in 1985. Put any allegiances to one side if you're from Norfolk or Wearside – Norwich playing Sunderland would have you screaming for mercy if you were faced with having to watch two and a half hours of live coverage between those two on BBC1 on a Sunday afternoon.

But it was so: two massively unfashionable teams playing in one of the only two live domestic matches shown on terrestrial telly that year. And my dad played up front for Norwich. Of course at the time I took it all in my stride. I only had one dad and he'd been a footballer for *ages*. Even before I was born Mick had gained his first England cap and that was basically the life I assumed every kid had – every other kid in the country watched their dad play football in the First Division of English football at the weekend as far as I was concerned. I also expected him to score. And I'd sulk if he didn't.

That was when he was playing for Southampton though. By 1985 things at home had changed quite considerably. To all intents and purposes, Mum and Dad had split up, which left us in what I can now look back on as a very strained household. We remained on the small stud farm just outside Southampton, and Mum did the horses, overseeing everything during the foaling season while Mick spent most of the week in Norwich. Mum did so because she's a good person and loved the horses. She certainly didn't owe Dad any debt of gratitude.

But Mick was (and is) a strange amalgam of characters. He always expected things to be done for him (he knew no other way of life aside from being a footballer), and people were willing to go the extra yard to please him. He has this sparkle that still makes people to this day make things happen for him. My life has also fallen under this spell, just like my mum's did back then.

In truth, Mick adopted a rather slapdash approach to monogamy. I hold no grudges – this isn't a score-settling process in which I hope to cleanse my tortured soul and blame anybody for what goes on in the world. It's just how things were, just how life was, and although things weren't great at home there was always football. Football dominated the vast majority of my childhood.

I remember the days just before dad went away to prepare for the Milk Cup final. We were walking across to the barn where we kept the mares and foals at feeding time and I asked him with a yearning that only a boy of my age and my upbringing could be capable of: 'If you score the winner in the Cup final, Dad, will you get a golden boot like Bobby has?'

'I don't think so, mate. This is the Milk Cup and we need to bloody win it first.'

This disappointed me immensely. Defeat hadn't entered my mind for a kick-off. Who *were* Sunderland anyway? My dad was a man completely at ease with the prospect of playing in a major Cup final at Wembley Stadium, but to me it was a *very* big deal. He was 36 by then. *Ancient* from my perspective, which was one shared by footballing people when you watched brief highlights of his exploits on the telly. But I knew he was brilliant. If you're still playing top flight football and making things happen while commentators like Barry Davies, Gerald Sinstadt and John Motson are describing you as a 'veteran' or 'an old warhorse' you're clearly very good. Remarkable almost. And he was. He couldn't run like he had as an England regular, but he'd adapted his game to bring younger players into play, and he extended his career far beyond the limits of others. Most of his best mates in football were washed up by the age of 32, yet here was me asking him about what we'd get if he scored the winner in a Cup final at Wembley.

He was my dad, and that certainly helped elevate him in my estimations, but he was also a brilliant footballer. He made things happen and he made people enjoy the game. He was an inspiration to teammates and fans alike. He's also a very abrupt and dismissive individual, which is not a particularly endearing feature, but very few successful people are 'nice'.

Especially people with his background. He'd done it all by that time: from becoming a hero at Southampton before failing horribly at Manchester City as the country's record-breaking signing (£350,000 was a lot of money back in 1977). He glossed that off to return home to Southampton, where he eventually became their record goalscorer, with 227 goals. When Saints finally sent him on his way, he eventually proved that the light still shone brightly by turning up at Norwich City, playing football as a hobby, training as often as he saw fit, and doing as he pleased.

The man does more hours today, but what he does still pleases him immensely, even when you'd think the opposite. He's grumpy and aggressive and perpetually demanding. We fall out often, and I'm aghast and infuriated for a lot of the time. In effect, he's lived his life in reverse – blessed with natural ability and a carefree attitude to any real work ethic in the first half while grafting tirelessly in the latter. He's a constant reminder of how life remains impossible is my old man.

Back in 1985, though, my question about getting a golden boot was all that bothered me. I'd become obsessed with my dad getting a golden boot like Bobby Stokes had.

Heroes never lived in your house, did they? They'd come round to visit and they'd make a fuss of you and then they'd leave, leaving you wishing for more. Just like my Grandad Reg did. Like Bobby Stokes did.

Bobby scored Southampton's FA Cup winner in 1976 and he gave Mick a moment that I don't think could ever be bettered. Dad was a Southampton supporter as a kid and he won the FA Cup thanks to Bob's goal. I can't speak for my dad, but that's all I ever wanted to do and, while my dad surely relished that moment of fulfilling a childhood ambition, Bobby went and got a golden boot for scoring that goal. It lived in his front room. I thought it was the best thing in the world.

That Southampton team in 1976 remain best friends to this day, regardless of how often or rarely they see each other. They picked up their FA Cup winners' medals from the Queen (she's not bothered to go back since) after beating Manchester United and they then all got pissed together for months afterwards. Obviously, it was a team effort, but Bobby was my first hero for both scoring the winner and having a golden boot in his living room.

Many years later, when I passed my driving test and Peter Osgood appointed me as Bob's driver to take him to charity football or cricket days, I still couldn't believe that Bob was my friend. I don't think anything gets better than that: my mate Bob and his golden boot.

Anyhow, on Sunday 24 March 1985 the Channon family and friends boarded a coach (a proper one as well – a 45-seater with a microphone at the front) at our home just outside of South-ampton. We were all there; Mum, my sister Nicky, Mick's brother

Phil and Auntie Liz, Grandma and Grandad Channon, Grandma and Grandad Medcroft, cousins, uncles, aunts and friends – it was a proper charabanc if my memory serves me right, and we left at an early hour and arrived in the coach park at the Wembley Stadium in high spirits, particularly Grandad Reg.

As we got off the coach Dave Allen, a friend of Mick's, dragged me aside and told me to follow him. The coach park at the old Wembley was enormous, and I thought we'd all be staying together, but as Mum and everyone else headed towards the Twin Towers a strange turn of events eventually found me and Dave standing outside the biggest set of wooden doors the world had ever seen.

There was a little door within them and Dave knocked and we waited. I didn't have a clue what was going on until a little old man in a black uniform and a cap opened the door and asked us what we wanted. He looked a day older than grass, and Dave struggled to get through to him over the considerable noise of the crowd around us.

'Can you fetch Mick Channon of Norwich City, PLEASE?'

The old man eventually nodded and went away. Some time passed until my dad appeared at the little door. I was told to step over the rather large step in the opening of these massive doors to get through to where he was.

'He's my son and he's coming in,' Mick said against protestations. 'Fucking let him in!'

And the old man in the uniform did so. The little door on the massive oak gates shut behind us to a cavernous echo. I immediately knew where I was. I'd seen the telly. I was in the tunnel of Wembley Stadium. Dad was standing there in a grey suit with a yellow flower on the lapel. I was standing there in an acrylic Norwich City tracksuit and a pair of trainers I hated. I hated them when I first got them and still hate the memory of having had to wear them to this day. They were from St Michael, a footwear range of Marks & Spencer, and they had Velcro fasteners. I wish my mum hadn't been such a stickler for purchasing off-the-peg trainers when I was growing up. A pair of Patricks or adidas would have made my crash helmet hairstyle more forgivable with hindsight. The eighties were a bastard to everyone.

'Come on, then!' The old man marched me about fifteen yards down the tunnel and turned me right, through a door. I walked in ahead of him and there was the entire Norwich City team, its backroom staff and all of the reserve players in the dressing room. The coach, Mel Machin, was standing next to a large tray of orange cordials with glucose tablets in them, sitting on a treatment table next to a pillar in the centre of the room. Mel wore a tweed cap and a tracksuit, a look even more fashionable than my trainers back in those days. He said, buoyantly, 'Now then, young man! You'd best have a drink and behave yourself!'

I was intimidated, scared and excited – in a pair of shit trainers.

I don't remember much of the following three hours of my life, but a few things will never be forgotten:

I remember drinking loads of orange cordials with glucose tablets in them out of plastic cups.

I remember sitting next to my dad, Asa Hartford, John Deehan and Louie Donowa as they got ready for the match. Louie was very kind to me and he wore Hi-Tec boots. I was obsessed by football boots during my childhood and Hi-Tecs were the best thing since Patricks at that time. Louie was like a kid himself, barely twenty, I guess, while the Norwich captain Dave Watson was a bit scary. As I was weeing in the urinal next to him just before kick-off he accused me of being more nervous than he was. (I'd properly got stuck into the orange cordials with glucose

Amazed, excited and walking out at Wembley

tablets in them, to be fair, and he'd noticed how many visits I'd made to the toilet.)

I remember that the old Wembley had a massive bath. *Massive*.

I remember the manager Ken Brown delivering a team talk.

I remember lingering behind my dad in the tunnel before we walked out. He was wearing a very strange turquoise tracksuit top.

I remember thinking I was going to follow my dad onto the pitch, but he didn't say anything to me – he probably had other things on his mind – so I self-consciously walked around the sand greyhound track in my trainers thinking about how shit they were.

The only thing I remember about the first half was not being able to see the first half. Wembley had four rows of leather benches for the coaching staff – one behind the other. I was in the second row behind Ken Brown, Mel Machin, the substitute John Devine and the physio, who was called Tim. I was only ten and a half.

I saw nothing.

I do remember my dad swearing at half-time, going for another wee and Steve Bruce ruffling my crash helmet haircut when we went out for the second half.

I remember Norwich scoring just after half-time. I remember that because I'd just been given an apple.

Asa Hartford had scored. Apparently.

I remember Mel Machin going mental when Dennis van Wijk gave away a penalty, and I remember Sunderland's Clive Walker missing it.

I remember being on the pitch and my dad picking me up and kissing me.

I remember feeling self-conscious as I was given the Cup in front of the Norwich supporters and a row of photographers and being told to hold it up in my shit trainers.

I remember after one lap of honour, my old man saying, 'Let's go round again, I'll never get another opportunity, so fuck it!'

I remember how happy everyone was.

I remember all the players getting pissed in a hotel.

What a day.

Before Mick went to the thirty-year reunion of Norwich City's one and only victory in a major domestic Cup final, an East Anglian film crew arrived at the stables to speak with him about that day. They set up in the owners' hospitality lounge and he went in to talk to them about it.

I was sitting at his desk, fiddling with the lot board that organises who will ride which horses the following morning and, after a mere five minutes, the director came out of the lounge and approached me.

'Mick says you might be able to help.'

'What with?' I replied.

The first kid on the pitch at Wembley. They all do it these days!

'Well, the trouble is, he can't remember the name of the captain that day.'

'What? He can't even remember Dave Watson?' I replied.

'To be honest, he's got trouble remembering most of the team.'

'Right,' I said, 'I'll write it down for him. Show him this and he'll tell you everything you want to know.'

And so I wrote the entire teamsheet out for him on the back of a declaration sheet that Mick had on his desk with the details of the following day's runners.

Now, I'm certainly not flagging this up as an example of how he's lost the plot through dementia. I say this because what happened thirty years ago really doesn't matter to Mick Channon. *He simply does not care.* Not a jot that happened yesterday bothers him. Once his memory is jolted, he's OK. He went to the reunion and was so happy to see everyone – even though forcing him to get out of the house and away from his horses took considerable effort, he *loved* it.

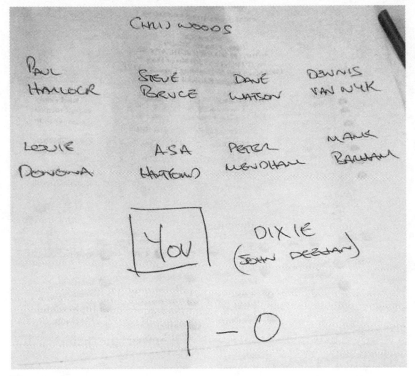

The team sheet

'Louie doesn't change, I had a right laugh with him, and Dennis is bald!' he joyously said when he returned.

'Oh, good,' I said. 'How's Asa?'

'Brilliant! Same as ever.'

'So you enjoyed it, then? Good, I'm glad.'

'It was a late one, though. Fucking hell, they wanted them "selfies" taken with me, and everything.'

'Well, it *was* a good day, Dad.'

'Yeah, but it was a fucking long time ago. I mean, why do people want to celebrate something that far back?'

An incredible outlook on life.

I've seen a million interviews with former footballers being asked to recall their big day at Wembley Stadium, and they usually say something along the lines of: 'It's a day I'll never forget.'

With Mick Channon, though, the most probable line will be: 'It's a day I can scarcely remember.'

He doesn't want to reminisce and he doesn't see the point in hindsight or nostalgia. He'll warm to it given the right circumstances, but I don't think he has a mind that can shift too far from the present or the future. For him, there's today and tomorrow or, more accurately, the day *after* tomorrow. Because that's when runners on the Flat are declared to run.

A remarkable man for his age. He only ever looks ahead.

NEEDLESS SHOUTING

EASTER MONDAY, 6 APRIL 2015

A mixed bag today as it coincided with my return from a fort-night on holiday. It was good to get away. While I don't work as hard as many, I'm always *at work*, and it can be mentally drain-ing when you live on site, enduring the disappointments and only ever briefly savouring success. Horseracing is a losing sport: you're lucky if 15 per cent of the horses win through the course of a year. Get your head around that one – I often can't.

Mick's got far thicker skin than me. He treats statistics and strike rates with complete contempt. That's the difference between us: where I fret over the disappointments and expend an awful lot of my time reflecting upon the agonies of defeat, the old man just forges ahead, finds an excuse or a fault (jockey, ground, opposition, even himself), swears for a bit and then wipes it all from his mind. That's a handy approach to have.

We had runners at Plumpton and Huntingdon today, and while our select band of jumpers have held their form as their season draws to a close, the Flat season has only just started and we've again been slow to get going. This is due in part to the quality of our early runners, as well as the location of our train-ing base at West Ilsley, ten miles north of Newbury. It's high up on the downs of West Berkshire, and since moving here Mick's runners have often been slow to find their feet in the early stages of the Flat campaign.

West Ilsley is a historic training establishment, responsible for producing thirty or so Classic winners when it was the realm of legendary trainer Major Dick Hern. The famous Astor family appointed the Major as its salaried trainer in the early 1960s, until the yard became the property of Her Majesty the Queen in 1982 and the success kept coming. Countless winners of the 1000 and 2000 Guineas, the Derby, the Oaks and the St Leger emerged from the old yard, and it is famous in racing circles for being one of the true powerhouses in the latter half of the twentieth century.

In 1999, in a bizarre and wholly unlikely turn of events, Mick Channon was 'invited' to make an offer on the estate by the Queen's then racing manager, the late Lord Carnarvon, due in no small part to Mick's rapid expansion in his first decade as a trainer. He had saddled his first winners in 1989, but by 1999 he was training a hundred horses out of three yards, one owned and two rented, in the famous racing village of Lambourn, some ten miles away.

As a result, Mick was one of the few expanding trainers able to service West Ilsley Stables at the time that it came on the market. He always says he offered 'too much for me and not enough for Her Majesty' but a figure was agreed and the deal was done.

West Ilsley has over three hundred acres of grass gallops, a huge array of equine facilities, an indoor ride, thirteen houses, three flats and two cottages, along with the trainer's home, Hodcott House. It's an astonishing throwback to the past – and rather reluctant to embrace the future. Every time one part of it is improved and modernised it seems as though another part falls to the ground. But while maintaining the place remains the equine equivalent of painting the Forth Bridge, it has character and charm and a record for producing champion racehorses that cannot be questioned.

The gallops all climb upwards towards the ancient Ridgeway peak that spans Wiltshire, Oxfordshire, Berkshire and Buckinghamshire. They are extraordinarily wide-ranging with stiff inclines that provide a proper test for horses, their fitness being more than assured. While Mick's time at Hodcott hasn't seen the same phenomenal success as Major Hern, he has had his moments, winning over sixty Group races and producing seventeen Royal Ascot winners.

The standout would probably be Samitar's Irish 1,000 Guineas success in 2013. Like the majority of the horses trained at West Ilsley today she was a cheap buy in horseracing terms, but she defied her price tag and her pedigree to be top class. Class horses are hard to fail with, and the gallops at West Ilsley more than play their part in the process. That's enough history, though.

Needless Shouting isn't classy but he is willing. He's owned by many of my friends in 'Lord Ilsley Racing', a syndicate run from the yard that specialises in buying cheap horses to race as two-year-olds before moving them on. Needless Shouting didn't win as a two-year-old but we figured that he was worth keeping hold of, and a rather good idea it was too.

Today, Needless Shouting is four years old, and having won twice over staying distances on the Flat last season he embarked on a juvenile hurdling career in the New Year. Despite splattering his jockey Andrew Thornton across the track at Doncaster on his jumping debut, he showed enough in his next two runs to suggest that he was a winner in waiting.

He won a juvenile hurdle at Plumpton today. What a lad. He jumped brilliantly and was never headed, winning by nine clear

lengths in a style that showed you how much he enjoys his life –
ears pricked and loving it. It was a joy to see, sitting at home in
front of the telly. I was too knackered after an overnight flight to
make it to Plumpton, and Mick had gone to saddle our runners
for the Radford family at Huntingdon.

Prior to his leaving, though, he delivered a 'pep talk' to one
of our two apprentice jockeys. This is a big season for Daniel
Cremin – he has rides at Catterick this week, the start of what
is a make or break year for him at the yard. This incident will
probably act as the very best insight into Mick's mindset, and
the reason he's been so successful in achieving his life goals. He
believes everyone shares his attitude to life, which is basically,
'Just go and be better than everyone else'. It's that simple, and
he's got almost zero regard for the insecurities that might exist
in others. His chat with Daniel Cremin underlined how little
empathy he has for others and how combative his approach to
everything he's ever achieved is at the core of his being.

A cockney lad, Cremin is conscientious, hard working, funny
and popular. Being an apprentice jockey means hard work, long
hours and copping a lot of flak when Mick's ever-simmering
temper boils over. Cremin comes into the office this morning, all
21 years and eight stone of him, head down and rigid.

'Right, you've worked fucking hard all winter and I'm trying
to get you going, boy!' Mick says from behind his desk.

'Yes, boss.'

'These jockeys in the north – they won't like you and they
won't give you a fucking inch!'

'Yes, boss.'

'Now you've got to get yer arse in gear and I can't do it for
you. You've got to take your chances because these are my horses
and that's why you're riding them. You've got to start fucking

showing me something, and that starts now!' This pep talk began to take on the familiar appearance of one of Mick's frequent bollockings. His voice was rising in volume.

'Yes, boss.'

'Right, now fuck off and remember what I've said, because those northern boys will eat you for breakfast!'

'Yes, boss.' The apprentice shuffled out of the office shutting the door behind him.

I sat there just looking at him. There was a pause, and then he added by way of explanation: 'I'm just worried that he'll get fucking intimidated.'

My idea of man management and Mick's idea of man management differ greatly. I've always been on to him, saying that the big stick is better used sparingly, while Mick's ever-present rage and explosions of fury render reason pointless. I know we'll never agree, because he thinks I'm suggesting some sort of team-bonding exercise in the Brecon Beacons with group hugs being obligatory at the end of every day. The thing is, every opinion that differs to Mick's is wildly dismissed and immediately banished to the opposite end of his spectrum. In his opinion, other people's opinions are 'bollocks'. In Mick's world, a conversation is an invitation to agree with him. If you don't, it ends up with a barney.

We aren't constantly at loggerheads – there's so much of what he does that I agree with – but when I disagree with him there's never a discussion and an exchange of views. I just nod and go along with him. Opposition would lead to conflict, and there would only be one winner in that contest. It's something that I admire about my younger brother Jack. He's 22 and sees the world entirely differently to me. He's got strong opinions and a youthful optimism about him. He believes he can change the world – and he certainly isn't scared of arguing his point. The only problem is that he challenges Mick over most of those opinions, and that's when the shit hits the fan and the shouting starts. Jack's problem is that he believes things can change, while my problem is that I know that they won't.

Two things of which I'm certain:

1) Jack hasn't endured the failures that I have.
2) Mick always has the final word. He's the boss.

And the boss does make me laugh. It was always said of my Grandad Jack, Mick's dad, that he made people laugh without intention, and Mick is very much the same. Bloodstock agents make him angry, for example. They are often calling up, interested in buying our promising horses. I remember with glee one morning when there was an offer for a horse called Chilworth Icon who had just won the Woodcote Stakes at Epsom on Derby day. He was clearly a very promising two-year-old and Mick was incensed when a bloodstock agent rang up and offered £30,000 for him. His anger grew as we drove towards the gallops, and by the time we'd reached the two-furlong marker he came out with a statement that sums him up perfectly: 'Thirty grand! I can't believe it. He must be worth a hundred! That's it, I've had enough with these bloodstock agents, they just take the piss and must think I'm an idiot. I'm not dealing with them any more. I'm not going to sell everything that's any good for peanuts. From now on we'll do it our way – *We'll fly our own fucking canoe!*'

I held it together for as long as I could but Jack, sitting in the back, couldn't. He started laughing so hard that I had to join in. Laughing at Mick when he's angry doesn't go down too well, which makes everything even funnier. One day Jack and I will call a horse The Flying Canoe.

But even in his foulest, most abusive moods, Mick is not particularly intimidating. He's regularly disheartening, and often soul-destroying, but his abuse still retains a sense of the bizarre about it. When he goes mental, he's utterly absurd. He can go completely off the scale, screaming, shouting, bollocking and brandishing a Basil Fawlty range of gestures that leave people open-mouthed in astonishment.

If the wheelie bins are left out for longer than he wants on collection day, for example, he can sometimes be on the verge of murder. Two minutes later, though, he'll attempt to have a laugh and a joke as if nothing has happened. This is clearly the behaviour of a man detached from reality, and only a successful footballer who had never heard the word 'no' from a very early age, or a racehorse trainer, would be able to get away with it.

That is no exaggeration either. Both professions can breed bizarre individuals.

Anyway, we went for a pint when he got back from Huntingdon this afternoon, at the Harrow in West Ilsley. It wasn't a bad day at all: Viva Steve had run well to finish second in the two-and-a-half-mile handicap chase, while Knock House won convincingly by over 30 lengths in the three-mile novice chase to follow his excellent run at Cheltenham. On top of that, I couldn't stop grinning about Needless Shouting's win at Plumpton. Needless Shouting – what a great name for a racehorse trained by my father.

Two years ago, Needless Shouting was a gangling, unraced, unnamed two-year-old colt. He was very cheap – four grand, in fact – and in that sense he fitted the bill perfectly for my syndicate's budget. He's by the stallion Footstepsinthesand and out of a mare delightfully called Ring The Relatives. It was the middle of 2013, early one morning on the summer gallops at West Ilsley. I was sitting next to Mick in the wagon as the unnamed two-year-old out of the mare Ring the Relatives galloped past us. Mick just says to me: 'Have your syndicate named that big bastard yet?'

'Yep, we voted on the name yesterday. It's a cracker.'

'What have you called it, then? I'm going to enter him at Salisbury.'

'Needless Shouting.' I waited for his reaction.

'Righto.' He was busy watching the rest of the horses work by the wagon and he'd quickly stopped listening as his mind wandered elsewhere. 'They've all gone all right them lot, you know! What's the name, then?' He drove on in the direction of the work riders.

'Needless Shouting.' I said.

He stopped the wagon. I could see him computing the information I'd just delivered.

'Needless Shouting? Needless Fucking Shouting?! Are you taking the piss out of me?!!!' His face reddened and I could barely hold my composure.

'It's a good name!' I countered. 'He's out of Ring The Relatives!'

'I don't give a shit! That's a fucking stupid name and I'd rather not run the fucking thing. It's an embarrassment!'

By this time his head was throbbing crimson, although my attention was quickly averted to his fist, which was banging the steering wheel, aggravating his chronic arthritis and making him lose the plot even more than I initially thought was possible. I'll also admit that starting to laugh didn't help matters.

'Needless Shouting?! Needless Shouting?! That's a ridiculous name!' he shouted.

'You don't do irony, do you, Dad?' I said.

'I don't even know what that fucking word means! All I do know is that Needless Shouting is a shit name for a horse!'

He finally relented on the naming issue (it took a month) and Needless Shouting has proved to be more than good value for the four grand we paid for him. He's not a star, but he's sound, willing and loves racing – perfect for a syndicate of enthusiasts and friends with a limited budget.

Before we finished our pints in the pub tonight, I received a text from a member of the Ex-Saints informing me that Bill Ellerington had died at the weekend. Now Bill Ellerington was Southampton Football Club's talent scout who had spotted Mick when he was playing for Wiltshire against Hampshire as a 14-year-old schoolboy in 1963.

Mick just looked at me when I told him the news. He went quiet for a moment. It was hardly a tragedy as Bill was 91, but he was a significant man to Mick. Bill Ellerington's intervention all those years ago put the wheels in motion that led to the levels of respect and adulation that Mick receives to this day from football fans of a certain vintage.

As for me, I'd known Bill Ellerington since I was a kid, and he once told me about his verdict on my own footballing ability when he was still watching games as a Southampton scout. Namely, the day he watched me play for Hampshire Boys: 'Yes, I remember you playing, Michael. It was a game at Eastleigh. I just wrote in my book, "Channon, No.8 – tall, lacks pace. *No*."'

Bill was a good judge of a footballer and he was dead right.

I was tall.

THE DAY THE WAGON DIED

FRIDAY 24 APRIL 2015

A day that reaffirmed the feeling that life is truly worth living. Friday mornings are work mornings at West Ilsley, meaning that we take the horses out of their comfort zones and ask them to go a stride quicker in their work. For many of the two-year-olds this means that they are 'off the bridle' for the first time. Essentially, we are asking them for maximum effort, almost replicating a real race, allowing us to assess which ones are ready and which ones need more time to strengthen before we try them again a little further down the line. Some that you suspect have true potential disappoint, but the great thing about working with young horses is the fact that we, as a team, are largely responsible for their attitudes, their work ethic, their appetite and their constitutions.

I've painted that picture with a broad brush, but you know what I mean. We need hardy, tough horses. Few of ours have classy pedigrees so we have to have tough nuts to expose any cracks in the opposition during a season. They have to work hard and have the right grounding. Mick's work ethic, his insistence on pitching them in against the best, and a willingness to 'keep the big boys honest' mean that, more often than not, we have disciplined juveniles who take their racing well.

We were sitting in the office just after six o'clock this morning when Sue Huntingdon arrived. A talented photographer, Sue spends many a work morning snapping the horses on the gallops.

'After the usual greetings, Sue approached Mick's desk as he was looking at the entry book. She seemed somewhat nervous.

'Erm . . . Mick, there's a chap outside who says he's a football referee and he's wondering if he can see the horses.'

Sue had met this bloke outside who was on a family break and had got up early to have a look around and had seen a sign for the stables. Sue only lives at the end of the driveway and had struck up a conversation with him. I can understand her trepidation in asking Mick if he could come up with us on the gallops. The 1000 Guineas is only a week away and this is the old man's traditional period of tyranny. His erratic behaviour increases tenfold and there is often a poisonous fog around the yard as his stress is taken out on others. I was on edge immediately, but this turned out to be the best visit we'd had in a very long time.

In walks a portly, bald-headed bloke, about fifty years of age, wearing a tracksuit top, football shorts . . . with a personality that flooded the office. Sue tried to introduce him but he immediately burst forth with bonhomie, bounce and excitement, all expressed in a Lancastrian accent nicked from the throat of Fred Dibnah. 'Bloody hell! Mick Channon – Man City legend!' he said as he walked in. Mick could barely muster a hello before he looked around the office and fixed his eyes on me. 'Bloody hell! I know you! You're Mick Channon as well! *Granada Reports*! I used to watch you on the telly! You're a television legend!' He grabbed my hand and nearly crushed it with a typical northerner's grasp before telling us that he was staying in a cottage in East Ilsley while on holiday with his family and how much he loved his racing. I knew more about his life after this opening five minutes than I know about those of many of my close friends. He was a complete whirlwind of enthusiasm – Mick was completely eclipsed by this bloke's character and just sat there open-mouthed – and I was shocked that anybody could remember my shambolic appearances on regional television over a decade ago.

He took the place by storm: 'I'm Adie. Eccles, I'm from, but I moved to Bolton twenty years ago when I met the wife. We're having a grand time, thanks, just staying in the village down the road and I thought I'd have a look around. We've got four adopted kids and we've fostered twenty-four others over the years, as it happens. I must say, Mick, this is a cracking place you've got here, people won't believe where I've been when I tell 'em. I'm a City fan myself, from Eccles, as I say. Is that Alan Ball?' He pointed to the large picture of Mick and Bally in their playing days together at Southampton that hangs on the wall behind the old man's desk.

'Yeah, that's me and him when I had hair, he was a Farnworth lad.' That was Mick's entire offering.

'I know he was! What a player! I'm a referee myself, met Howard Webb. I had dinner with him. And now I've met Mick Channon! City legend! The lads won't believe it! I love my racing. What are you up to this morning, then? The wife and kids are still in bed, but it's too good a morning to lie around . . .'

I left the office to trot the horses in their warm-up in the indoor school smiling to myself. What a great lad. Today would be a good morning. The mood on work mornings is usually dictated by the first thing that happens. If a bin hasn't been taken in after Thursday's collection day a cloud quickly descends. If a horse is late in because it needs the farrier to re-plate a shoe, a cloud quickly descends. If a horse is seen pulling out with straw in its tail, another cloud quickly descends. Mick, more often than not, latches on to the most trivial of matters, expands it, turns it into a disaster and launches a volley of rage that often sets the tone for the rest of the working day. But when an uninvited Mancunian lunatic arrives and starts jabbering on at him in the office and gives him no choice but to listen . . . well, that's a recipe for a good morning.

Even when the gallop wagon dies.

To be fair, it's been on its last legs for quite some time now. For the last ten years it's been bounced, crashed and thrashed across the Berkshire downs by an unremitting, ceaselessly driven driver. Probably the worst driver I've ever known. It's played host to some of the most improbably formed opinions and discussions I could ever imagine and witnessed some of the most fearful bollockings ever heard.

The gallop wagon has also known some great days. It's overseen the preparations of Flashy Wings, Silca's Sister, Majestic Roi, Music Show, Youmzain, Halicarnassus and Samitar ahead of memorable days of joy on the racecourse. It was also witness, along with Alan Ball and I, to the sight of Mick bollocking a traffic cone.

That was eight years and three days ago, to be precise. Bally was with us when one of the two-year-olds veered out and kicked a cone placed to mark a fresh strip of ground during a morning's exercise.

This made Mick angry.

As a consequence, he thought it would be productive to give the cone a good kicking across the gallops to teach it a lesson. Unfortunately, due to the sand-filled base, this hurt him so much he went even more mental. Bally cracked up and I joined in.

'He's completely mental!' Alan said between gasps as the old man hobbled and swore his way back towards us.

'What are you two fucking laughing at?' said the old man when he got back in the wagon.

'You!' said Alan. 'You're not right! Is the cone sacked?'

'Fuckin' right it is!' The old man broke into a smile. Bally could always defuse his rage. At times they lived in each other's pockets, but they could live without each other as well when their footballing lives flung them apart. Basically, though, they loved each other. Days without laughing about or mentioning Bally are few and far between.

Alan died eight years ago today, but it seems more like three. He was a massive figure in all of our lives and has left a gap that still hasn't been filled. It simply can't.

Today, though, with Mick's refereeing, foster-parenting Mancunian sedative in the back, smiles were abundant. The gallop wagon roared up the hill towards the winter ground on Hodcott Down as Lancashire banter abounded. The wagon, however, clearly wasn't in love with life. This wasn't a healthy roar; this was a guttural, mechanical vomit that twisted everyone's face into a wince. The wagon seemed to be devouring itself and complaining in rage at the same time, and then it just stopped at the three-furlong marker next to the woodchip gallop.

'Don't sound too healthy, Mick!' said our guest. 'Have you had problems with it before?'

'Yes. The problem is, the fucking thing is fucked,' explained Mick. 'However, you can kid it into action by driving in reverse.'

He's right as well. I think we have the only vehicle in the country that is capable of reversing faster than it can go forward. And so our guest was treated to a trip in a Land Rover Discovery that morning and spent 90 per cent of the journey travelling backwards. And he loved every minute of it.

The end is nigh

'I bet this is how Aidan O'Brien oversees his work mornings,' I remarked.

'Fuck off,' said Mick.

It was a good morning all round. Of the two-year-olds a colt named Jaadu jumped out at us and won his gallop quite convincingly. He's uncomplicated, good-looking, sound and straight. From what I've seen of all of them – from the breaking and endless hours of trotting and hacking around the indoor school through the winter – he's the most talented we've got, along with a filly called Kassia.

Good horses aren't hard to train, and Jaadu and Kassia are no different. We'd have about 80 of the 5,000 two-year-olds entering training in 2015, and it's more through hope than expectation that we base our chances on unearthing a star. That's what keeps us going, really – young horses can be anything, with no idea of what they cost or what their parentage is. Mick Channon, like Alan Ball and Wayne Rooney, came from a council house, and that's what we rely on for the majority of our youngsters – a diamond in the rough. That said, Jaadu and Kassia are among the most expensive we've bought. While the vast majority of our two-year-olds are either homebreds or cost less than twenty grand, Jaadu at 90,000 guineas and Kassia at 120,000 guineas are the crown jewels.

We'd just seen Jaadu go three lengths clear of his fellow two-year-olds, and we'd had to abandon the wagon, which was left smoking like a tramp after the second lot on the summer ground. We had to call the yard for a lift home.

Jaadu has been entered at Ascot for his debut on Saturday, and we've got a stressful week ahead of us: Bossy Guest and Malabar will run in the 2000 and 1000 Guineas respectively the following weekend, so nothing could be going better than it is now in terms of the wellbeing of the horses or the hope that we have a good season in front of us.

I don't think the gallop wagon will see the end of the Flat season though – November is a long, long way away.

'Thanks, lads! I'll be off now!' We'd returned to the yard and Adie was shaking hands with the pair of us. 'The lads will never believe this one when I get back. *Two Mick Channons, two legends*!

I don't think the word 'legend' applies to me, though – certainly not in television, and I'm struggling to remember any other life achievements that have covered me in glory.

GRANADA TELEVISION

SEPTEMBER 1998 – SEPTEMBER 2002

As a kid, I'd always dreamt of being a footballer. The fact that I wasn't good enough was a bitter blow at the time, but one that prompted me to go to university in Bristol, fall off a roof, and then go to university in Liverpool before eventually getting a proper job.

That said, I don't think working in television could ever be referred to as a 'proper job'. I'm sure the industry has changed since the late 1990s and early 2000s, but I found it to be an extension of university life. Indeed, Granada TV in Manchester was an extraordinary place to work, with a cast of characters and a series of challenges that make me smile to this day.

My employment at Granada didn't last for long, and it's easy to see why, really, when you consider the three main work-related tales I'm not particularly proud of:

A live broadcast on Liverpool FC's open-topped bus tour of the city in 2001.

Setting fire to the newsroom.

Causing Kevin Keegan to storm off live on air. (At least I think he did.)

Initially, getting my foot in the telly door was a doddle. I'd tried the usual avenues, like reading the media section of the

Guardian newspaper and sending off my CV as everyone else does, but my television experience certainly came up a little short when it was written down on paper: washing up in pubs, a stint laying concrete, stacking shelves in Asda and working as an usher in a bingo hall in Southampton hardly made me a stand-out contender for a career in the media.

My sport science degree from Liverpool John Moores University hardly pointed towards one either, so Plan B was to call the old man. He'd had a vastly successful career in telly, the high-points being a summer arguing with Brian Clough and mispro-nouncing Gary Lineker's name on ITV during the 1986 World Cup. As a result, Mick was very good friends with Bob Patience, a producer from ITV Sport who was influential in all manner of successful programmes in the 1980s. So, with a phone call made and a favour granted I was summoned to do a fortnight's work experience at Granada Television's 'MUTV Lifestyle' department in the autumn of 1998.

These were the days of the satellite television boom of the late 1990s and there seemed to be opportunities for anybody, regardless of their experience or ability, to make dreadful tele-vision. And we made some truly dreadful television. I had zero experience, apart from setting the family VHS recorder to tape the entire series of *The Thorn Birds* for Mum when I was a kid. Little did I know it then but that proved to be more than enough expertise to work in satellite television. Everything we did was crap, and I'm fairly certain that none of it was watched.

On the plus side, for the whole two weeks, they paid all of my expenses, which worked out at about £3.80 a day – my tram fare to and from Mum's house in Timperley, near Altrincham – and I was eventually offered a six-month contract as an assistant researcher, which worked out at £8,500 a year. I snatched their hands off. Within six months I was working for Granada's sports department as a researcher in the main building on Quay Street and on a whopping £12,500 a year. Heady stuff.

I'll not bore you with my unrelenting, prodigious and effort-less rise up the television ladder (basically, if someone went to Sky, everyone below got promoted) but eventually, and for some unfathomable reason, I ended up in front of a camera at Bury's Gigg Lane. It was Tuesday 5 September 2000 and I found myself doing a live interview with the club chairman about the contin-uing financial struggle in the lower leagues.

A tough gig.

Granada Reports went out to the entire north-west of England. I don't know what the potential viewing figures were but I estimated at the time that it was 'a lot'. I was very nervous. My biggest mistake was an attempt to say the word 'perennial'. I remember shakily holding what seemed to be a very heavy microphone, sweating like an extra out of *Tenko*, taut in every fibre of my being. The disaster that unfolded went something like this.

Gallery: 'Cue Mick.'

Me: 'Yes, and welcome to Gigg Lane ahead of Bury's League Cup clash against Crewe Alexandra. Alongside me [sashaying to one side] is Bury chairman Terry Robinson. Terry, thanks for joining us on *Granada Reports*.'

Terry Robinson: 'A pleasure, Mick.'

Me: 'Now, Bury, financially have been perennumonollol . . . perenniallal . . . perenniallalgical . . . preren-anal . . .' I went bright red, froze and almost started crying. I don't know what happened after that. All I remember is going back to my girl-friend's house and swearing on every single member of my fami-ly's life that I would never show my face in public again, let alone on Granada's regional news programme. That was me done with being on the telly as far as I was concerned. The only problem was that me being on the telly was sort of written into my contract. I was a television sports reporter by then. When that's your job, it's sort of expected that you not only report, but that you report *on the telly*. I was getting £15,000 a year for this too.

Things didn't get a lot better after that, but my ability to fuck things up became cult viewing. Not for the regional television viewers in the north-west of England, but for many of my work colleagues in the newsroom at Granada. I hated it, they loved it. I was obliged to do it, though. In spite of being a very outgoing person in familiar company, I quickly learnt that professionalism and a certain amount of self-confidence was required to be on the telly. I had neither. I remember a girl in the graphics department at Granada asking me the following: 'What *is* that look on your face when you first appear in vision as the studio hands over to you on air?'

I had no idea what she was on about. 'What look?'

'This look!' She showed me a freeze-frame that the graphic department had gleefully taken of me standing on the touchline at Tranmere's Prenton Park. I looked mental.

'Oh that? That's my, "Don't say cunt" face.'

'What?'

'That's me telling myself not to say "cunt" live on air.'

'What?'

'Well, when I'm listening to my intro from Ali in the studio and just before the PA in the gallery says, "Cue Mick," all I can think about during the whole process is the fact that someone has put me on the telly and that, if I wanted to, I could say the worst word in the world at any time and there would be nothing that anyone could do about it.'

'You want to say "cunt" live on air?'

'No, but that's where my brain takes me. I have nightmares of doing it all the time.'

That's not a great starting point for a career in television, is it? In 2001, I was chosen to cover the UEFA Cup final in Dortmund between Liverpool and Alavés. Myself and a cameraman called Steve Brookes were dispatched to Germany, told to find some stories and send them back to Manchester. Just the two of us, with all the camera equipment, accreditation and a hotel booking. That was it. I remember seeing the BBC *North West Tonight* team at the airport. They had presenter Gordon Burns, a director, a researcher and two camera operators with them. Granada just sent Steve and me. It was a good trip, though: we did a few interviews with fans in the city and met up with former Liverpool player Jim Beglin. Not only did he help us out with a feature on the game during the build-up, he even helped us to carry all of the equipment across town to the Westfalenstadion. League and Cup Double winners make excellent camera assistants. We cobbled our way through, Liverpool won the match in extra-time, and we headed back to the hotel for a few drinks before flying back to Liverpool the next day.

Our hotel was the press base for the trip and one drink became two and dominoed relentlessly on from there. We ended up in the company of several ex-Liverpool players – class players, *proper* drinkers – and I enjoyed the evening tremendously until I woke up outside of my hotel room at three in the morning. My sleepwalking habit had returned again, and I was forced to run the gauntlet of avoiding detection as I trotted across the hotel's open-plan lobby in full view of a still vibrant bar to request a spare room key.

In just my pants.

The following morning, Steve and I were in the hotel lobby wondering where the rest of the media were, only to realise that the press bus had left for the airport without us. A mad scramble saw us grab a taxi and sprint through Dortmund airport to board our flight. Luckily, the flight was delayed on our behalf, although the Liverpool manager Gérard Houllier and his squad looked less than happy with us as we made our way to the back of the plane.

I was also chosen to be the *only* reporter on the team's open-top bus parade a few days later. Granada TV was a Liverpool stakeholder, with something like a 9 per cent interest in the club. Hence the plane delay, hence my presence as the only interviewer on the bus, with the footage relayed to other media companies via a helicopter satellite link overhead.

This was trickier than I had imagined. Liverpool had won three trophies that season and I figured it would be a doddle to get the interviews that everyone wanted. Michael Owen was the main man at the time and he was at the back of the bus with his teammates Jamie Carragher and Danny Murphy.

'A few words, Michael?'

'No, I don't feel like it. Carra will do it.'

'Jamie, incredible scenes here today?'

'I don't feel like it, mate. Murph will do it.'

'Danny?' I was almost on my knees at this stage.

'Who's it for?'

'I'm from Granada but this is going out to—'

'No, I'm not doing it – anyway, I did an interview for the BBC before we got on!'

All three of them erupted in hysterics.

It was humiliating, although I did receive the sympathy of plenty of colleagues who were watching the footage coming into

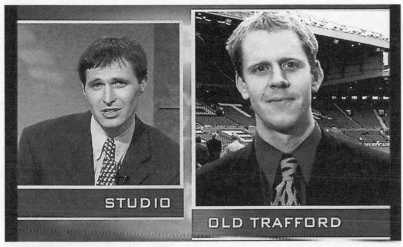

The beginning of another live disaster

their respective stations. One chap from the BBC pulled me at a press conference a few days later and said it was hilarious, while a Sky reporter said that he thought I handled it particularly well. Apparently, as I turned away I just looked into the camera and said, 'Suit your fucking selves and fuck this job,' or words to that effect. I died on my arse on that bus, and only Jamie Redknapp came to my rescue by asking people to help me out.

I hated the job.

Over the next couple of years I was fucking up live broadcasts all over the north-west of England with unerring regularity.

I got a verbal warning, not only for jokingly suggesting a fight with *Coronation Street*'s Jez Quigley (Lee Boardman) on the touchline at Old Trafford prior to a Champions' League game against Bayern Munich, but also for displaying a betting slip regarding who the pair of us thought would be the first and last goalscorers. I think I was going for 'banter', whereas what was really sought after by others was 'professionalism'.

I was sent into Manchester city centre to interview happy England fans after David Beckham scored England's penalty winner against Argentina during the Japan World Cup of 2002. However, because the match in Sapporo took place at nine o'clock in the morning, licensing hours had been relaxed and all-day drinking meant that the city centre resembled a war zone by mid-afternoon. So we abandoned the town centre on account of the riot police, the smashed shop windows and the street brawls and decided to head to Wilmslow, a slightly more refined part of Greater Manchester, where we thought we'd come across slightly more level-headed, sober members of the region who could provide us with positive feedback and accentuate the feel-good factor that our producer wanted for the three-minute live broadcast.

The scene in Wilmslow was similar to the one we'd left in the city centre, except for the fact that Greater Manchester Police were stretched so thin that there were fewer of them in attendance. We found a pub that was just about sane enough and decided to conduct an interview with a few lads in the beer garden. We had little other option because we were due on air at 6.15 p.m. and we'd spent much of the afternoon trying to find people who could speak, in somewhere that wasn't smashed. The clock was ticking.

Therefore our anchor, the late, great Tony Wilson, was forced to link to me live from the studio with little or no idea of what I'd come up with or what to expect. I was in the same boat. I was petrified of any references to Maradona's 'Hand of God' and especially the Falklands War from my hastily assembled guests.

Tony Wilson: 'Street parties everywhere and a street party just up the road from Mr Beckham's home, where are we? Oh, you're there, Mick!'

I was sitting drinking a pint of Guinness. I think I was trying to embrace 'lad culture' that was doing the rounds at that moment in time.

Me: 'Hello, Anthony. I'm here at the Coach & Four in Wilmslow [cheers ring around from my rowdy crowd of guests]. I didn't have to look too far for my "expert" panel, and alongside me is Justin. Justin, what do you reckon?'

Justin: 'It was fantastic, because we deserved to win because we hate the Argies!' [more cheers all round].

Me: 'It wasn't really about the performance, was it?'

Justin: 'The performance was shit, but I think it was fantastic!'

I could see my career slipping away far quicker than the actual broadcast seemed to be taking. I thought we'd be taken off air any second, but to my horror the gallery allowed it to lurch towards its awful conclusion. I attempted to wrap it up.

Me: 'Well, that's all from us, if our *Granada Reports* viewers will forgive us for Justin's "expert" opinions, I'll just leave it to the fellas to take it away . . .'

Crowd: 'NA NA NA! NA NA NA! NA NA NA, NA NA NA NAA NAA, ENGLAND!'

I was swamped by a series of head ruffles and backslapping. I held my head in my hands.

Tony Wilson: 'Thanks, Mick, yep, really good job there . . . Mick Channon trying to control the public of Wilmslow.'

I had no idea if we were still in vision or not when the lad next to me slammed a small bag of powder onto the table next to my Guinness.

'Fancy a line, Mick?'

A nightmare, but then again, most of it was. I often look back with bemusement at the number of opportunities that came my way, and they *kept* coming my way despite the fact that I never could quite get to grips with the thought that TV was a career. I took everything for granted back then, and always teetered on the brink of disaster.

Setting fire to the newsroom wasn't great either. On Saturday evenings the sports department would take it in turns to compile the goals and match incidents from across the region and play them 'down the line' to other regional companies. If Rochdale played at home to Plymouth, for example, the highlights would be edited up and played down to West Country TV for their evening news bulletin.

And so it was that I was standing on the balcony of Granada's newsroom anxiously smoking a cigarette awaiting the arrival of a courier bike who was nail-bitingly late ahead of our deadline to West Country TV.

The editor appeared at the balcony: 'Mick, it's here!'

I scrubbed the fag out on the brick wall and ran into the edit suite across the large open-plan room. We'd been slapping down goals, a missed penalty and were in the middle of trying to find a sending off when there was an almighty commotion outside of our soundproofed suite. I was stressed and narkily opened the door: 'What the fuck is going on out here?'

I froze. In front of me were two Granada security personnel with CO_2 fire extinguishers putting out a fire in a waste paper bin and blowing paperwork from half a dozen desks across the newsroom in the process. The fire wasn't an inferno, but the place resembled a ticker-tape parade of office documents as the plastic bin formed a puddle on the carpet and the place reeked of melted desk laminate. I probably should have dropped the cigarette before I ran into the newsroom. I probably shouldn't have dropped it into a waste paper bin. I didn't sleep well that night. The fire brigade were duty-bound to attend the scene and it cost something like £11,000 all told. The place stank to high heaven and fellow journalists had their deskwork rearranged across an area of about thirty feet. I wasn't popular on the Monday morning when they returned to work.

Following Keegan out at the Dell, 1981

Written warning.

Fair enough, really.

21 October 2001 was a Sunday. Preston North End played host to Manchester City in League Division One (now referred to as the Championship) with Kevin Keegan, City's new manager, returning after a professional and personal disappointment as England manager.

I'd known Kevin for ever, since he'd become a great friend of my dad's as a teammate, firstly for England and latterly at Southampton. Kevin was always very kind to me: he'd given me a pair of his football boots and even one of his England shirts. A good man.

By 2001, though, he'd clearly had a hard time in the aftermath of his departure from the England job and was trying to rebuild his reputation with Manchester City. Granada TV decided to cover this north-west derby live and I was given the role of pitch-side reporter responsible for the pre- and post-match interviews.

It wasn't a good day for City. Having taken the lead, they were beaten in the second half as Preston came back to win 2–1. Kevin took it very badly. During the adverts, I was told to pre-record an interview with Kevin that would be played out in the post-match discussion. They wanted two minutes, tops.

Me: 'Kevin, a disappointing day for you—'

Kevin Keegan: 'Very disappointing. I look around our dressing room and I see players on a lot of money with big reputations, and for that set of players to put in that sort of a second-half display is unacceptable. We've been made favourites to win this league and, while on paper we have the squad to justify favouritism, the truth is that some of them need to buck up their ideas. With ten games gone, I won't accept it any more. There's no passion, no leadership and no spirit. I've told them what I expect and I'm not getting a response from them. They've had every opportunity to impress me and I'm going to have to start making changes . . .'

He went on and on and on, the disappointment pouring out while I had the director screaming in my earpiece to wrap it up because Kevin continued for well over our allotted two minutes: 'Mick, you're going to have to stop him because we won't be able to use that. We'll have to go live and keep it to a minute because there's only three minutes until end credits.'

So I stopped Kevin in mid-sentence and explained that we'd have to do it live. He was very flustered by this time and clearly very upset. I had one minute to nail down exactly what he'd said. Like a professional journalist would. I got my cue and here it came. Me: 'Kevin, a hugely disappointing afternoon for you and having spoken briefly, is it the case that you feel as though some of your players have had their chance and missed it?'

Kevin was clearly taken aback by the nutshell I'd presented him with. He snapped: 'No, that's not what I said to you. That is a stupid question! A stupid question! And the reason you've asked me a stupid question is because you've been asking me stupid questions since you were *five*!'

I can only liken that moment to falling off my bike as a kid. Everything was in slow motion for a few seconds and then returned to real time after impact. And I wanted my mum.

I don't remember exactly what happened next but I know I couldn't speak. I just sort of stood there, 'goldfishing'. I'm not sure when we went back to the studio or how, although I remember a chap called Chris Bird, City's 'chief operating officer' telling me I was 'out of order!' and ushering Kevin away.

All things considered, I don't think I was cut out to be on the telly.

2000 GUINEAS DAY

NEWMARKET, SATURDAY 2 MAY 2015

In 1988 I watched Southampton beat Arsenal 4–2 from the Milton Road terraces at the Dell. I was 14 and for Saints to beat Arsenal so entertainingly and so convincingly was a real thrill. I don't remember much about the match apart from the feeling of happiness when I got the bus home. Nobody liked Arsenal back then. What sticks in my mind more than anything was the weekly phone call with my dad. As with most father–son relationships, after the hug and cuddle phase is over our only means of communication involved discussions about football. It was stilted and sometimes awkward, but at least we had a conversation point.

'All right, mate?'

'Yeah, good, Dad. Saints won.'

'I saw that. Did they deserve it?'

'Yeah.'

'The kid got a hat-trick. Is he any good?'

'He's all right, I suppose, but they were all tap-ins. He didn't do much else.'

'He scored a hat-trick! He must have done well.'

'He did all right, Dad, but he's probably a flash in the pan.'

That's me, 14 years of age, a real authority on football and describing Alan Shearer as a 'flash in the pan'. What a judge.

Me and Bossy Guest

Today, Bossy Guest ran in the 2000 Guineas, the first Classic of the Flat racing season. To win a Classic is everything. To win a Classic race – the 2000 or 1000 Guineas, the Oaks, the Derby or the St Leger – can define a racehorse and ensure that his or her name attains immortality, with breeding rights to that individual ensuring the financial rewards can be truly astounding. To win a Classic establishes a pecking order in the modern day and, with records reaching back as far as the eighteenth century, immortality for horses, owners, trainers and jockeys.

It's a big deal.

It's horribly cold and I'm not expecting much, to be honest. Bossy Guest has been a star throughout his career to date, having already won over £160,000. Last month he got our season off to a flyer by winning a valuable sales race at Newmarket to add another £56,000 to his pot and ensure that his owners, the Guest family, have another year financially taken care of, with the rest being a bonus.

But that race was a sprint over six furlongs – the 2000 Guineas is two furlongs further and against the best horses in Europe. As ever, though, Mick was insistent that he should go for the Guineas. I told him straight, only a week ago, that he was fool-hardy to waste a race against better-bred and far more likely opponents. 'He's a sprinter, he's not good enough and he'll never stay a mile,' was my assessment.

'Yeah, but he's rock solid, he'll switch off and relax through the race and, fuck it! – it's the 2000 Guineas. There's only one Classic at this stage of the season, and if we win he'll be a stallion,' was Mick's dismissive reply.

I remember thinking he was a complete idiot.

The betting market agreed with me as well. Bossy Guest was 50/1 but odds of 100/1 were readily available if you looked about. A complete no-hoper against seventeen opponents who had far better claims to make an impression than Bossy Guest.

This is a very big deal for us. We finished second with Zafeen in the 2000 Guineas of 2003 and he went on to become the European Champion Miler that year. Back then, though, Mick was riding the crest of a wave and finished the season with his highest career total of 143 winners from his squad of almost 200 horses. Talent oozed out of the yard back then and I spent the year visiting with a film crew as we followed his season, making a documentary for Channel 4. Mick gave me more access than he would to any other film crew. His reaction to Zafeen's second in the Guineas, and further footage as he screamed at both horse and jockey in the blanket finish in Goodwood's Sussex Stakes, were worthy of far more exposure.

That was probably the high point in Mick's life as a trainer. He doesn't have the same quality of horses these days, and younger, more fashionable trainers have arrived on the scene. On top of that, Mick neither appeals to nor courts new clients as readily as he probably should. 'I'm not going to spiv people to have horses with me. I want them to come because they want me to train their horses. I'm not going to hustle punters.' That's how he views the situation, although it does irk him. He wants to compete against the best all the time, but it's ultra-competitive, particularly when he doesn't have the sort of backing that he once had.

That's life, but I can see that it makes him rally even harder when people write his horses off. I don't think it's healthy for him, but if you took the challenge of training away from him, he'd be on the wrong side of the soil very, very quickly.

Today, he's more fiercely driven than I can remember him ever being. He rages against the world a lot of the time, and I often find myself resenting his aggressive, forceful spirit almost as much as I admire it.

And that's where Bossy Guest mirrors his trainer's zest for competition. Tough, game and talented, Bossy Guest arrived as a yearling – an angry and brutal individual. He's very genuine, though: unaware of his flaws and willing to throw himself into any battle regardless of the odds against him. His front legs are shocking, but thankfully they are the only pair he has ever known. He's not a good walker, he trots badly, but canters just about OK.

It's when he gallops that things really click into place.

Where his seasonal reappearance less than a month ago was electric, running in the 2000 Guineas was an altogether different prospect. I watched the race in the veterinary shed behind the saddling boxes at Goodwood while Mick was on hand at Newmarket. From the stalls Bossy Guest was outpaced and towards the rear of the field for much of the race. They went very fast and, just over a quarter of a mile from the finish, jockey Charlie

Bishop shook the reigns and Bossy Guest went forward, making up three, four, five lengths in a matter of strides. The rising ground saw him still gaining on the front-runners and he looked dangerous for a second or two. I started shouting at the telly.

And then he flattened out – although he never stopped.

Fourth in the 2000 Guineas with a rank outsider, and it wasn't a fluke. Bossy had covered three of the last four furlongs quicker than any other runner in the field. He'd stamped himself as a class act with a bright future. A bit like Alan Shearer did against Arsenal in 1988.

And I'd written him off. The old man was right again.

The bastard.

1000 GUINEAS DAY

NEWMARKET, SUNDAY 3 MAY 2015

While yesterday's 2000 Guineas saw me watching the big race from the veterinary barn at Goodwood, the fillies' Classic found me craning my neck around the 'Bathwick Tyres Paddock Bar' at Salisbury Racecourse before I legged Charlie Bishop up on a horse called Wagstaff five minutes later.

I couldn't see much. Salisbury is a traditional old country track, and one of my favourites, but the telly in the bar adjacent to the parade ring is almost as old as the city itself. In black and white, I could only make her out at the two-furlong pole, and it was even trickier to see the finish at Newmarket because it appeared to be snowing as well.

Unlike Bossy Guest's remarkable effort, Malabar's fourth place today was solid but initially left me feeling slightly deflated. It was a tremendous run but we never seem to win the 1000 Guineas – it feels like a jinx for us. In 1999 Queen's Logic, undoubtedly our greatest ever horse, was a massive favourite. She had murdered every horse she'd faced as a two-year-old, winning the Group 1 Cheveley Park Stakes by seven lengths. On Guineas day the next spring though she was withdrawn on the morning of the race with a foot infection, and retired shortly afterwards. Flashy Wings followed four years later with similar claims to Queen's Logic only for sixteen hours of rain to scupper her chances before Nahoodh needed a stepladder to win having been boxed in on the rails two years later and finishing on the bridle. Add to that Music Show winning her race on the far side only for the field to split right across the track with the winning group on the stand side and you'll get a picture of the frustration involved.

Too much detail? Probably, but the long and the short of it is that we've spent too much time cursing luck, and that doesn't solve a thing. Only winners matter, and we are perennial losers. That said, Malabar's defeat today brought with it no hard luck stories. She was outpaced throughout but will be better over further, and I was left to ponder what might have been while meeting Mick's former teammates from Shrewton United.

Salisbury Racecourse is always well attended. It's a proper track with knowledgeable Wiltshire enthusiasts, and there are always plenty from Hampshire up for the day as well – seldom does a day go by on that course where I don't bump into people who played with my old man when he was a teenager at Shrewton. What a club that must have been in the early 1960s. I'd like to conduct a poll on people from the surrounding area who didn't play either with or against Mick when he was a kid. It's all I ever hear about when I'm there – they must have had a squad of about 500 players; the village leagues of Wiltshire must have been immense. I do enjoy it, though. Wiltshire people are almost always funny, whether that's their intention or not.

Needless Shouting ran again today – not much to shout about, to be fair, but he does try. A two-year-old filly called Sixties Sue made her debut this afternoon and ran well to finish third for Norman Court Stud who own and bred her. She'll win a little race, although she is far from being a star. We're just waiting for one to jump out at us and give us the chance of taking on those at the sport's top table. The Richard Hannon stable filled the first two berths, and they are very much at the top.

Richard Hannon Senior was on hand at Salisbury. He's just handed over control of the business to Richard Junior, who won the trainers' championship in his very first year last season. That sort of thing can make anyone feel inadequate. Their assistant trainer is a multiple champion trainer in his own right, whereas ours is a lad from Southampton with only a degree in sport science, a half-decent work ethic and nepotism on his CV. I'm glad our horses don't know that.

THE NEW
GALLOP WAGON ARRIVES

TUESDAY 12 MAY 2015

The old wagon had to go. A sad end to an old warrior, but enough was enough. Today represented the dawn of a new era, or so we thought. It's silver, the roof doesn't leak, the seats are relatively clean, and it not only goes in reverse it goes forwards as well. Mick was devastated to lose the old wagon, but the brand new Land Rover Discovery certainly made the morning easier. We could head out to the gallops expecting rather than hoping to actually get there.

However . . .

I've just got back from Norman Court Stud in Wiltshire. It's about six miles east of Salisbury, and was Mick's pride and joy before he sold it to finance the expansion and redevelopment of West Ilsley seven years ago. He's now a director at Norman Court rather than the owner, and has stayed on to help the stud's new owners, Patrick and Tania Trant, long-time friends of Mick's since his playing days in Southampton. It suits all parties, with Mick also having another say in another business. I wasn't supposed to go to the stud today, but I got the call to come and fetch Mick about an hour and a half after he'd left.

'Can you come and get me? The car's fucked!'

'What?'

'The new car, the fucking thing won't go forward!'

At this point I was tempted to suggest it was no different to the old one, but thought better of it because he was obviously seething. I headed out and fetched him, convinced it was merely an operational error – man bamboozled by machine – but no. They reckon the gearbox has gone. A good effort that – one day and it's knackered already.

SPEEDING

SATURDAY 16 MAY 2015

A rare Saturday, as I was on 'Daddy Day Care'. We didn't have any runners in the north so I accompanied the old man to Newmarket where Elidor won a decent handicap for our primary owners, Jon and Julia Aisbitt.

Elidor is decent. He was a Royal Ascot winner a couple of years ago and has maintained a high level of form ever since, although he's hardly a prolific winner. His consistency tends to give him little chance with the handicapper – a tedious and oft uttered excuse by everyone in the racing game.

The one runner meant that we were away without fuss before the last and we listened to the football on the radio all the way around the M25 and along the M4 back to Berkshire. Saturday afternoons are always good for driving – there was nothing on the roads as we made good time for home and a pint in the Harrow.

There were some cars on the road, obviously. In particular, there was a blue Volkswagen Passat. Not that I noticed it. I apparently hadn't noticed it for a good two miles as it followed me with its blue lights flashing. The old man woke up as I pulled over to the hard shoulder. 'Bollocks,' was all I said.

'What's up?'

'Police.'

'Whatever you do, don't admit that you were speeding.'

'Don't admit I was speeding? I *was* speeding and they'll know more than me about exactly what speed I was doing, Dad!'

'Don't admit to anything,' were his final words.

Now, while I was obviously annoyed with myself and overcome by the inevitable trepidation of being asked to sit in the back of an unmarked police car on the hard shoulder of the M4, another part of my brain was trying to process exactly what sort of a planet my old man lives on.

I shuffled into the back seat of the police car, having to slide over a banana, a packet of Hula Hoops and a tuna sandwich in the process, and all of a sudden the moment seemed a little less intimidating.

'Do you have any idea as to why we have stopped you, sir?'

I thought about what the old man had said to me. 'Speeding,' I said.

'Do you have any idea what speed you were going at?'

'No.'

'Do you have any idea how long we were following you?'

'No.'

'You passed us at Reading services, and you were clocked at doing ninety-three miles per hour.'

'Oh.'

'What's the national speed limit on the UK's motorways, sir?'

'Erm, seventy.'

'Can you explain why it took you three miles to notice us in your rear-view mirror, sir?'

'Erm, I was concentrating on the road ahead.'

'Right. So you were driving well in excess of the national speed limit and failed to see us in your rear-view mirror.'

'Erm, yes.'

'Now, I could take this matter further, sir. Travelling at that speed brings with it a mandatory three-point penalty. Have you got points on your licence?'

'No.'

'Do you want points on your licence, sir?'

'Erm . . . no.'

'Well, luckily for you, this equipment on my dashboard is a camera that I should have had pointing at the windscreen but, fortunately in your case, I had it pointing in the wrong direction.'

'Oh.'

'Your face looks familiar, sir. Do I know you from somewhere?'

At this stage a thought flashed through my mind as I recalled Adie, the Manchester City and Granada TV fan. Was it possible that this copper had also seen me on *Granada Reports* fourteen years earlier? I doubted it and, besides, I didn't think this was either the time or the place for being absurd. 'I don't think so.'

'What do you do for a living?'

'I work with racehorses.'

'That's probably it, because I used to work the beat in Lambourn.'

I'm hardly a renowned face in the racing village of Lambourn, so perhaps he *was* a fan of regional television in the north-west, but I chose not to pursue the matter. 'That'll probably be it,' I said.

'Right, well, on your way, and please make sure you are up to a decent but *legal* speed before you rejoin the carriageway.'

I was something of a nervous wreck after this process, and rather pathetically said 'sorry' and 'thank you' before fumbling my way out of the car. I got back in the driver's seat of Mick's Merc.

'Well, did he do you?' he asked, as I put my seat belt back on.

'No, he had the camera pointing the wrong way.'

'You've had a result, then. You didn't say that you were speed-ing, did you?'

'Of course I did, Dad. They're not fucking idiots, you know.'

'I don't know about that,' he said, laughing. 'Right, let's go for a pint.'

THE CRASH

WEDNESDAY 27 AUGUST 2008

I was completing an edit for Highclere Thoroughbred Racing in my office above the yard at West Ilsley. This was not only a hefty project that involved five weeks of filming across the country; it also meant that my foundering company, Piccolo Productions, was finally on the up. After almost four years of struggle, and several bouts of anxiety and depression, I was on the way to clawing back almost fifty grand of debts and had a decent run ahead of me.

I was quite good at it as well. I knew about horses, which is always a good start when you're filming them and providing DVD updates on a major syndicate's string, and I also knew when to bother irate trainers and when to leave them be. Also, I'd finally learnt how to make a few quid out of the game. You cannot pay camera crews and commission edit suites at five hundred quid a day and make any money yourself with the sort of contracts I was negotiating. What you do is get your own gear – a decent camera, some laptop-editing software – and do it all yourself. Such tools were relatively new on the market (or at least they were to an ignorant plank such as myself), but with optimism came both growth and the development of rudimentary production skills. I'd been on camera, directed and produced telly before, and had spent endless hours telling people what to do in edit. Now I had myself to organise and, like I say, I was quite good at it. Not brilliant, but efficient for the sort of market I was servicing.

At about six o'clock in the evening, I had a call from my stepmum, Jill. She sounded very worried. Had I spoken to the old man?

I hadn't.

He'd left Doncaster's yearling sales at lunchtime and still hadn't got back. The M1 can be a bollocks at the best of times so I wasn't unduly concerned and, besides, I was doing a sound mix for Highclere. I'd been concentrating on that all afternoon. At about half-six I headed down to the Harrow for a pint and a chat with the locals. I was in good form. I felt like I was finally making a success of myself, independent of any external help, and in buoyant mood. I remember everything that followed.

Pete, the landlord, said that Caroline in the office was on the phone. I took the call and was told that the police were on their way. I calmly left my pint, got in the car and drove the mile back to the office. When I got there, I was told to head over to the big house. The day seemed to have taken on a very grey complexion.

I arrived in the kitchen to find Jill shaking. Not the sort of nervous tension of a concerned wife and mum, the sort of savage panic that nobody wants to see or deal with. Mick, Jack and Tim Corby had left Doncaster just after midday. It was now seven o'clock and the traffic reports had said that there was a major incident on the M1 just south of Nottingham and that the motorway had been closed. I'd rang both the old man and Tim when I was in the Harrow but neither of their phones had responded.

Caroline then came in, ashen-faced and shocked: 'The police are here.'

I walked to the door and saw a policeman and a policewoman crunching towards me across the gravel driveway. A bizarre, almost comical thought struck me: 'Fuck. A female copper is always present when someone has died on the telly.' I went numb, Jill began to sob. The kind of sob I cannot describe. Sky News was on the little telly in the corner of the kitchen, Jill was crumbling against the Aga, the policeman was asking the sort of questions they ask in *Eastenders* and *The Bill*: 'I have some information on Mr Michael Channon and Jack Channon of this address. Are you Mrs Channon?' I was leaning opposite Jill on the chopping board. The chopping board makes up an 'island' in the middle of the kitchen. It's a lovely kitchen. Jill just collapsed into me. I mean *collapsed*. Again, I just cannot explain the emotion I was witnessing. I held her up to prevent her hitting the floor and just waited for the news as Jill went mental: 'MY BOYS! MY BOYS! OH NO, MY BOYS!'

'Mrs Channon, there was a serious incident on the M1 just after two o'clock this afternoon involving a silver Mercedes. We have reason to believe that Mr Channon and your son were in the vehicle.'

I just said, 'Are they dead?'

'They are in intensive care and, as far as we know, they are in a serious condition. We have no more information than that at this current time.'

The policewoman moved forward. She looked so caring and so perfect, but Jill kept on going. I just couldn't let go, stop thinking, or stop analysing the situation: 'What about Tim? What's happened to Tim? They were with Tim.'

'We are currently trying to contact Mr Corby's next of kin. Until we do, we can't give you any more information.'

This was the most mental situation I'd ever been in. We all have family, we've all lost someone close to us, but this was imagining you've lost two people in your family, but not actually knowing whether you have or you haven't. I knew, though, from the policeman's expression, that Tim was dead.

Tim Corby: a man of many faults and many vices but so many virtues and sweet insecurities. He was brash, loud, uncouth and straightforward. But not really. Tim was just a great bloke. He drove Mick mad, constantly moaning about jockeys, questioning entries; he was a frustrated trainer who no doubt thought he'd do the job better himself. But that all said, he was my old man's mate. He'd been his mate for over thirty years, and if you've been my old man's mate for over thirty years, you're all right by me.

That paragraph probably took you longer to read than the consideration I gave to the gravity of the situation at the time, though. I just wanted to know what to do next, although all I remember about the next stage of the process was that it was light when the coppers arrived and dark when we set off for Nottingham University Hospital.

In the interim, I'd had at least a bottle of wine and nicked all the fags Joe Tuite had. Joe was the old man's assistant at the time, not popular with the staff, but a man who I'll always hold in high regard. He sorted a driver and assured me that the yard wouldn't stop operating as usual. Mad, really. Why did that seem to matter?

Our stable lad 'Fat Ali' drove us, and I was on the phone all the way, mainly to my sister Nicky, who made sure we avoided the M1 courtesy of the information we had from her telly.

We headed up the M40 from West Ilsley, stopped for fags at Warwick services (I know), took the M42 and skirted the M1 via Derby. It was while we were on the M42 that Nicky called to deliver the news that made both Jill and I frantic. Sky News had announced that the incident on the M1 was due to a fatality.

While all but concrete evidence had told me that Tim had died, the direct line to the hospital provided to us by the police continued with the same updates on the condition of Mick and Jack: 'Critical but stable.'

How did we know they were telling the truth? We were stone cold in our analysis of the situation by now. Would they really tell you on the phone if Mick or Jack had died? *We actually had this conversation.* Would they just keep you in the dark if the worst had happened to prevent a meltdown before you got there? I thought that they probably would.

I'd splattered myself across a patio in Bristol and got myself in a right old mess only thirteen years before and knew the clarity of thought that you experience when adrenaline and fear take hold. Likewise, I remember that conversation on the A52 entirely. We were half an hour from the hospital by then and I simply didn't know what we'd discover when we got there.

It was dark and warm when we arrived at the entrance of the Accident & Emergency unit of Nottingham University Hospital. We said who we were and a woman was summoned. I can't remember what she looked like but she was efficient and caring. We were taken to a room. One of those rooms they go to in an episode of *Casualty*.

'Mrs Channon, your husband and son arrived separately. Mr Channon arrived first in the air ambulance at four-thirty and your son about an hour later by ambulance.

'Your son is in the high dependency children's ward under observation before we run some more tests and some more scans. He's very lucky that he's so young and healthy, but he will be OK in time.

'Mr Channon is in ICU. He's received some very serious injuries to his head and jaw, has a badly broken arm and several broken ribs. He has punctured his lung and we have inserted a chest drain to help him. He's also fractured several vertebrae. Tonight is critical, and before we give you any assurances as to the chances of recovery I would like to stress that we are as satisfied with his condition as we possibly could be under the circumstances.'

We were shocked, confused and impatient people. Jill was the first to speak: 'I want to see them *now*.'

'I'M NOT GOING TO CHANGE!'

MONDAY 8 JUNE 2015

Accidents happen all the time.

Bossy Guest fell over today. It's the week before Royal Ascot, and to say that he was well would be an understatement. His fourth place in the Guineas showed how talented he is and, to be honest, had the Royal Meeting taken place last week it wouldn't have been soon enough. The trouble with training racehorses is that they are fit, well and fed high protein foods. I've yet to know one who has turned to drugs, smoked cigarettes or gone out on the piss before eating a kebab in the cab on the way home. These are fit, tight, primed horses – that's what they are bred and trained for.

Plus, Bossy Guest is the ultimate enthusiast. Monday mornings are notoriously fraught, with the fit horses having a Sunday to rest as the sick, lame and lazy are assessed to see if they can rejoin the string on the following day. Consequently the fit string are bouncing with life on a Monday morning, and Bossy Guest is usually the freshest of the lot.

There's a road crossing to the gallops at West Ilsley, and on the way home Bossy Guest decided to leap into the air and whip round all at the same time. He slipped and landed on his side on the tarmac, as his regular rider Tango disappeared onto the grass verge. Bossy's right flank has cuts and grazes all along it. His right knee was weeping and I'm not far off it too. This is not what we need so close to Ascot, and the cuts, although only superficial, might become infected unless we're very careful. A nightmare we could well do without. There was lots of swearing. To be fair, there's been lots of swearing for what seems like ages now.

Charlie Bishop was sacked last week after a two-year-old lost the plot at Chester, and he was sacked again this week because of a ride he gave a particularly troublesome filly at Nottingham.

During last Friday's work morning it was our youngest apprentice jockey Paddy Pilley's turn to get two almighty bollockings, one after the other. We were working two-year-olds up the grass and Paddy pulled a young horse to the outside very early on in a piece of work and Mick went off his head. Thirty seconds later, not satisfied with the first bollocking, he stopped the wagon and gave Paddy another bollocking because he was angry with him for getting so many bollockings.

Getting a bollocking for getting so many bollockings must surely be a sign that the bollockings aren't working. I think that even Mick possibly picked up on this bizarre scenario because he ended up screaming, 'I'm not angry with you, I'm fucking frustrated because you're such a cunt!'

This sense of the bizarre has been on a loop for well over a month now.

Alan Ball used to do bollockings: really mad, passionate, dressing-room explosions of rage. I saw quite a few of them, particularly when he was manager at Portsmouth, where he'd assembled an outfit of really wild players who gave him sleepless nights aplenty.

Mick was in his last year of professional football at the time, and I'd regularly go training with him and spend time in the dressing room on match days. I was 11. It was a great time, watching my old man enjoying football for what it was and laughing at Bally's constant headaches that a group of players nicknamed 'the Gremlins' caused him on an almost daily basis.

I was with Mick Quinn, who played alongside the old man in that Pompey team, at Lingfield on Friday. Quinny trains a few horses these days, alongside his growing career as a presenter on talkSport radio, and he's a bloke I love spending time with. While Quinny had a runner in the last, I was there to saddle Sixties Sue, who promptly won at the third attempt just to prove that we're not doing everything wrong. As they went to post, Quinny said he was going to have a score on her so I gave him a tenner and off he set to get the best price.

Having roared her home he went to pick up our winnings and returned with £360. Could we work out our share? Could we bollocks. We just looked at each other and fell about laughing – me a failed footballer, and Quinny a former footballer, unable to divvy up three hundred and sixty quid. At least I had the same brains of a footballer even if I lacked the talent.

I remember one day when I was playing in his youth team at Exeter, Alan Ball called me over after training and explained what he wanted and how I could help myself. That voice: 'Son, there should be no highs or lows in your performances, no inconsistencies and no excuses. It's down to you to get things right throughout everything you do. On Saturday you scored and did one or two bits and pieces that show you've got plenty of talent, but you're either a nine or a four out of ten. And there are far too many fours.' I can hear Bally saying that even today. Back then I knew he was right, the only problem I had was that I simply couldn't do anything about it. Bally, when he wanted to be, was an inspirational man-manager.

Mick, though, is as erratic as my football was.

When he's a nine he's the greatest man in the world to be around. The trouble is that his fours are probably twos, and they are beginning to blur my ability to remember the last time he was in good form. There's constant complaint and constant blame, with very few people benefiting from any of it. The young jockeys are nervous wrecks and far too frightened of failure than they are hopeful of success, and this is certainly played out in their performances and ultimately our results.

While all this is going on, Mick acts as if he's an innocent victim. I'd love to make the point that he's steering the ship. He's making the entries, booking the jockeys and training the horses. The trouble is that this will just lead to another confrontation, which usually ends with him screaming, 'If you don't like how things are, you can always fuck off and find another job because I'm not going to change!'

And I'm on his side.

ROYAL ASCOT

TUESDAY 16 JUNE – SATURDAY 20 JUNE 2015

I shan't insult your intelligence by pretending that I returned home from the Royal Meeting every evening to update this journal with a sober analysis of what went on during the most competitive, stressful and social week of the calendar year.

I'm writing this on the Sunday after at West Ilsley Cricket Club, whom I'd stupidly agreed to play for before the week began. I was rather surprisingly asked to open the batting upon my arrival when, if I'm honest, I was barely able to open my kit bag. That ought to illustrate simultaneously how desperate WICC were for players today and how much of an alcoholic onslaught Royal Ascot can be. We're currently 39 for 5 (Channon 13) and I'm sitting under a tree reflecting on the bold showing of our horses, the disappointment of not making the headlines and how I could completely miss a straight one (it did keep low, but nausea and blurred vision might well have played a part).

Unless you're from one of the big yards with the class horses, you really should approach having runners at Royal Ascot rather like a ten-year-old should view a trip to Loch Ness: hope rather than expectation is called for, or you're in for a demoralising experience.

There are a few things about the pomp and ceremony of Royal Ascot that I'll always resent. For example, the guilt-inducing process in the car park of turning people down when they ask for owners' and trainers' badges as you make your way in. As with most things in the modern world, charm and chancing no longer make a dent. The halcyon days of blustering into the owners' and trainers' entrance and getting half a dozen badges for 'our drivers (there's three of them), John Smith, his wife Agnes, and their poodle Derek' are long gone. They want emails, faxes, I.D and money if our badge requirements exceed the limit of six owners per runner. Consequently, I'm often out of pocket before I get in. I'd like to think I'm a generous person to those I know well and I'd do anything to help a friend – and that includes buying badges for people who have done well by me in the past. It's the people who you have only a vague recognition of from past car park experiences that really grate my arse. They've turned up in a morning suit, a waistcoat and a top hat and then ask you for a badge to get in. Did these people accidentally turn up at Ascot unaware that there was a day's racing on? 'I'll see what I can do,' is my usual response, while my brain is screaming, 'Fuck off!' As with much of the etiquette associated with Royal Ascot, though, my frankness is uniquely British: understated and seldom expressed.

On the Tuesday we only had one runner in Opal Tiara, a homebred two-year-old filly who has exceeded all expectations by winning impressively on debut at Wolverhampton before finishing a bold second in a well-regarded conditions race at Beverley. On the Monday morning prior to the meeting, our finance director Gill 'the till' Hedley and her partners, in the form of brothers Clive and Keith Potter, were Opal Tiara's sole owners. By Monday lunchtime, however, Qatar Racing's Sheikh Fahad had bought into half of her. Every horse has its price and Opal Tiara had hers. It was a boost for everyone though, because

Gill, Clive and Keith copped a few quid but they also had a new partner who wanted the best for both himself and the horse. Opal Tiara has enormous potential as well, and we're still all in it together. She's raw, talented and a star to train. I barely paid any attention to her in the two months of trotting and hacking her round the indoor school through the winter. She really was that easy to get going as a yearling.

For adults, Tuesday of Royal Ascot is a bit like Christmas morning for kids – just louder and eventually messier. Everyone arrives in the owners' and trainers' car park beside themselves with excitement, the picnics are laid out and the champagne poured. It's the beginning of an onslaught that remains unabated until the final race of the meeting on the Saturday evening.

The whole scenario is daft, really, when viewed at face value. Take the pomp and ceremony, the stupid clothing, my nagging uncomfortable shoes that have refused to work with me since I bought them in March, and the presence of the Queen out of the equation and I'm staggered that so many people think that Royal Ascot is such a noble and acceptable event. Put it this way: if you spent a week drinking from the back of a car at midday and then went from pub to bookmaker, pub to bookmaker, pub to bookmaker, pub to bookmaker, pub to bookmaker, pub to bookmaker and then went back to drinking from the back of a car until nightfall, you'd be held up as a scoundrel and a bounder of the highest order. Not only that, they'd encourage you to seek counselling.

Do it in a top hat, though, and it's fine.

And then there are the sandwiches. Fucking hell, the sandwiches. The sort of bland, futile and seemingly eternal sustenance that leaves you hankering for a wheat allergy long before the Wednesday is through. That sort of diet is just not normal.

Thankfully, I work in racing and there is something else to focus on. Sure, I like a drink, but I honestly believe that attending such an event as just a social exercise would tip me over the edge.

Before the week started, I'd made a vow to make sure I drove Mick to the races after we'd exercised the horses every morning. This wasn't through duty or professionalism but through self-preservation, because he's probably the scariest driver on the planet. It's not only his complete lack of patience, his total and unrelenting inner rage and the phone calls he takes, it's the fact that he has zero awareness of other road users. Last year he drove to Glorious Goodwood, and by the time we arrived I was a nervous wreck. I'd witnessed two near misses and he hadn't seen a thing. *Not a thing.* He even asked me the obligatory rhetorical question as to why other drivers on the M27 were pulling alongside him and gesturing the wanker sign once he'd got off the phone: 'What's wrong with people on the roads? People are so *angry* these days. I just can't understand it.'

I was so scared that I couldn't even speak. That was the same day that he pulled across the entrance to the car park as we headed home while on the phone to an owner, blocking the stream of taxis trying to get in to pick up their customers. When a stream of abuse came his way, he simply said, 'Hold on a minute, sir,' wound the window down and shouted, 'Fuck off, ya dickhead!' before putting the phone back to his ear and saying, 'Sorry about that, Prince Faisal, some person was in my way.' And off we went.

For a while I tried to analyse how a footballer of such vision back then could lack so much awareness of what's going on around him today, but, having said that, he couldn't even detect the look of absolute terror on my face that he'd caused prior to our arrival. I suppose he's just a different person these days, with so much on his plate. Everything he deals with is internal – entries, declarations, owners, jockeys, results and the state of the ground around the country. He takes everything on without trusting or delegating anything. As far as he's concerned 'delegation' is what happened to Burnley last season.

But when the pressure is at its highest, I've vowed to insist on driving from now on.

Opal Tiara ran in the last and she was superb in the Windsor Castle Stakes, a Listed race for colts and fillies over the shortest distance of five furlongs. She was drawn on the stand side in stall 24, and with 28 runners the outcome of the race can often be dependent on where the early pace is. In recent years there has been an influx of international runners attending the Royal Meeting, and an American trainer, Wesley Ward, has had huge success with his juveniles, who go quick and hard from the moment the stalls open. As it happened, the American horse, Ruby Notion, headed for the far rail and Opal Tiara, outpaced early on and with little else to race with, flew home on the nearside to finish a very promising seventh – a winner on 'her side'.

The vast majority of a life in racing is trying to accentuate the positives and looking to the future – all the time hiding the disappointments as best you can while dreading the pitfalls ahead. At that, I'm not the greatest. You can probably tell.

The Wednesday was our big day, with Bossy Guest lining up in the Group 3 Jersey Stakes trying to improve on his fourth in the 2000 Guineas in May and belie our fears that throwing himself on the road last week had affected his chances. He's a brute of a horse. I'm not entirely sure whether he's just incredibly tough or incredibly stupid, but he didn't let us down. He's a horse to admire.

We had to beat the Richard Hannon-trained horse Ivawood, who was half a length in front of us in the Guineas. He was carrying a five-pound penalty on account of winning a Group 2 last year and, on paper, we stood every chance of overturning the deficit as a result, although the bookmakers didn't think so, making Ivawood an outstanding favourite in the race with Bossy Guest an 8/1 chance.

As fate would have it, though, we were left licking our wounds while ignoring Bossy Guest's scabs on his nearside flank, having been stopped inside the final two furlongs by a tiring Ivawood and Lucky Kitten, who had set a blistering pace on the far side. Bossy was only beaten by a length and a half and Charlie Bishop, freshly reinstalled from his latest sacking and riding in his first ever race at Royal Ascot, was almost in tears at the luckless passage he'd endured. He'd followed the favourite and suffered because of a rival who simply had an off day. Nobody could see it coming and, despite closing all the time, once he'd found daylight the race was over and our big chance had gone.

Bollocks.

Not the sort of comment you'd utter in front of the Royal Box, no doubt, but that's how I felt. Having a winner at Royal Ascot is becoming harder and harder.

Kassia was up next in the Group 2 Queen Mary Stakes over five furlongs for two-year-old fillies, and she ran a cracker to finish fifth, while Lincoln had no luck in the Hunt Cup with the pace yet again developing on the far side, leaving him with no chance of ever getting involved.

That was our big day, really, and with all three running well but very little to show for it, it summed up the majority of our days at Royal Ascot.

There was little to speak of on Thursday too, which will primarily be remembered for a hedgehog waking me up at three in the morning. While my sleepwalking has often got me into bother, this was no such occasion: I was woken by a scratching along the skirting boards in my bedroom. I even Googled 'Can hedgehogs climb stairs?' and, believe it or not, they can. Either that or one of the lads in the yard thought it would be a funny prank to play on the boss's son. (He's never a popular person, the boss's son, is he? But not one of them met my accusations with a look that suggested guilt.)

If you take nothing else from this book, I can confirm that hedgehogs, when the mood takes them, are capable of walking into a kitchen, through a lounge, up some stairs and into the master bedroom of a two-bedroom cottage in a racing yard. It was probably my fault for leaving the back door open.

On Friday the shit truly did hit the fan as Jersey Breeze found no cover again from a stand-side draw and paddled home in the Group 3 Albany Stakes for juvenile fillies. Charlie Bishop received the mother of all bollockings as Mick's rage hit an all-time high in the unsaddling enclosure. There's little point in revealing the details but it was a dreadful day filled with blame and bitter disappointment. In the background I was trying to paint on a smile and console her owners. Mick lasted until about half-seven in the car park before his toys truly came out of the pram, and he was in the car and gone inside thirty seconds. I was as embarrassed as I was angry, but I don't think too many people noticed. This was the car park after racing at Ascot, after all.

We had only the Saturday left, and the realistic chances of making headlines were receding rapidly. Sixties Sue was outclassed but ran a blinder to finish midfield in the Chesham Stakes, and Divine finished likewise in a typically ultra-competitive Wokingham Stakes, leaving me to find solace in a few pints of Guinness in the owners' and trainers' bar.

I was glad to get home, to be honest, although I don't hold out much hope of even enjoying success in the cricket today. We're about to take an early tea having been bowled out for 92. Apparently I'm opening the bowling as well, but I don't feel like the sort of bloke anybody should turn to for a spark of magic in any sporting sphere right now.

'SHUT THE DOOR'

THE DELL, AUGUST 1994

My top three footballing moments:

1. A hat-trick for Cheadle Town away to Trafford FC in the North-West Counties League in 2002.

2. No goals but a brilliant all-round display for Hampshire Under–19s Colleges at Wide Lane, just near to Southampton Airport. I don't remember the opposition.

3. Two goals for Fulham's reserves in a friendly at Kingstonian FC's ground in 1993. I don't remember the opposition.

That's not a great list of achievements on the field of play, is it?

I thought I'd throw them in at the top of this chapter because it's something I want to write about without in any way suggesting I was any good at football. We've all sat in the pub and heard about the bloke who had a trial for Bournemouth, Coventry, Fulham or Southampton – I'm that bloke – but with the enduring regret that the manager didn't have a clue, or that injury meant he missed out on a career at the top level, thus robbing him of fame and fortune (I'm definitely *not* that bloke).

I was *moderate*. Better than a pub player but not good enough to make a career out of football as a professional. I want to make that clear from the kick-off. Because I've been dreading this bit. These are memories that haunt me.

My childhood is to blame, and the hope I carried through all of it obviously deluded my judgement of what went on in the real world. To possess ambition and enthusiasm is one thing, but, when I look back, there's a lot to be said for perspective and pessimism too.

Let's start with the hat-trick against Trafford FC in the North-West Counties League. I was brilliant that night. A free-kick in off the far post for the opener, before a great turn on the halfway line and a brilliant left-footed pass out to the left led to a lung-busting run into the box and a drilled, side-footed finish from ten yards as the cross arrived. The penalty to seal a 3–1 victory was a formality. It was a game that probably only I remember. To be fair, there were probably less than 300 paying customers there that night (definitely, in fact), but I was a different class.

To put the word 'class' into perspective here, I think I ought to point out that this was Division Two of the North-West Counties League, although it did contribute to me being voted Player of the Month for February of that year. For that, I was presented with a magnificent silver salver – engraved and everything.

I used it as an ashtray. You probably get my point.

The game for Hampshire Under–19s Colleges at Wide Lane, just near to Southampton Airport, again saw me at my very best. The fact that I cannot recall the opposition, however, again renders it a particularly unworthy highpoint in a typically overblown memory bank of personal achievements. It's true though, I was head and shoulders above everyone else that day. And by a country mile.

As for the two goals for Fulham's reserves at Kingstonian, that in itself is something of an exaggeration in terms of its status. In 1994 Fulham didn't even *have* a reserve team. They were a club so skint that they didn't even have goals at their training ground. In fact, they didn't even have a training ground. They used the west London fire brigade's playing fields and had a squad of seventeen players who washed their own training kit. So the game at Kingstonian's ground was made up of those few players Fulham had who didn't get a regular game, a few tri-allists and a load of kids in a kit that was so old I think Johnny Haynes first wore it back in 1960. The age range of this team was between 15 and 35 but, again, I was outstanding. That was the night that I could have become a professional footballer. Seriously, it almost happened for me. But Robbie Fowler went and fucked it all up.

Stuck in Division Four of the Football League, Fulham were a team with diminishing crowds, diminishing ambitions, bugger all prospects and fuck all future. They were dismal and I reckon I fitted right in. In training I did well for the two weeks before my game at Kingstonian. The goals were pairs of traffic cones nicked from the M25, and the assistant manager, Ray Lewington, would judge when the ball went out of play because there were no lines marked out, unless we played on the rugby pitch. He was a good bloke, Ray Lewington, a good coach too and a fella who responded to my letter asking for a trial by phoning me up personally. He'd played against the old man so obviously that opened a door for me to a certain extent, although I know that Mick didn't have any contact with him prior to my arrival at the west London fire brigade's playing fields.

That's why I felt so free: that and the fact that the 'goals' were nicked from the junction just off the motorway; and that training took place in a park. Because it was totally unprofessional, I felt totally at ease in that environment.

My two goals at Kingstonian (against another team I cannot remember) took place on a Friday evening. Fulham's first team were beaten on the Saturday after that, and when I arrived for training on the Monday, Ray and the manager Don Mackay pulled me in afterwards to say we'd 'sort something out' at the end of the week. There wasn't any training on the Tuesday because there was a League Cup tie away to Liverpool in the evening, and Wednesday was a day off. I thought I'd be a professional footballer by the end of that week. I was concreting the stable floors in Lambourn for the old man at that time, so a change in career, even if it meant I'd have to wash my own training kit, would have been most welcome.

But there was a fly in the ointment.

Robbie Fowler scored five goals for Liverpool on his first-team debut against Fulham the following night. The next few training sessions were awful, and they only got worse from then on in. Players were bickering, the team was losing, and all was not well. It became very clear, very quickly, that Fulham were a club in even worse shape than I initially imagined, and that their downward spiral showed no signs of ending very soon. Don Mackay got sacked shortly afterwards. That, to all intents and purposes, finished me at Fulham.

That was a disappointment, but I didn't ever stop trying, and opportunities kept coming my way. For the next bit, adopt a high-pitched Lancashire accent:

'Right, gentlemen, welcome back. This is where the season begins.' Alan Ball in the car park of the Dell, home of Southampton Football Club. 'You can put whatever you want into pre-season training. You can put everything in or hold a bit back for yourselves if you like – but I will be watching. As will Lawrie, as will Lew, as will Dave and as will Ray. I've never held anything back and I've never asked for anything more than 100 per cent. You give me that and I'll be fair with you. I'll be running as well, so don't get behind me or you'll be in trouble!'

There was laughter and wisecracks, although not from me because I was standing there as well, with a Southampton training kit on and a pair of crap trainers that I thought would do (crap trainers must be a family trait). I was so nervous and so overawed that I can still remember it to this very day. This was me, pre-season training with Saints: Iain Dowie, Ken Monkou, Jeff Kenna, Francis Benali, Paul Allen (who played in the 1980 FA Cup final for West Ham – my first ever FA Cup in front of the telly), they were all there. The same group of men I'd screamed on to Premier League survival on the last day of the previous season in the Bobby Moore Stand at Upton Park. They drew 3–3 that afternoon and it was the best day I ever had following Saints.

But I wasn't following them today – *I was with them*. Not only them, but also *the One*. Standing less than ten yards away from me, by the whitewashed trellised door to the players' entrance, was Matthew Le Tissier.

Now, I don't wish to sound fawning or over-dramatic, but this was one of the greatest men on the planet to my nineteen-year-old self. As good as Jimmy Case, whom I'd worshipped before his departure just three short years earlier. Le Tissier was even more of a hero than Joe Corrigan, my first footballing idol at Manchester City when I was barely four years old. Le Tissier *was* Southampton as far as I was concerned.

'Right,' continued Bally, 'you all know what is expected of you and you all know what I want. If you've got a problem, come and see me. If you don't agree with me, come and see me. I'm an open book and I don't hold a grudge, so make sure you do the same. *My door is always open!* Right, today will be steady enough and Lew will show you the route. Do your best and enjoy it.'

And Bally's assistant manager, Lew Chatterley, led the way. Up Southampton Common, across Glen Eyre Road, into the sports centre car park, down the hill, past the boating lake that Nicky and I would row across on our days out with Grandma. It was filled in by then, though; a tragic consequence of health and safety mania. We ran on, down the tarmac access road below the paddy rice-style football pitches, then uphill towards the municipal golf club, around the course's most northern point and back down towards the Dell via Hill Lane, past King Edward VI School – acute paranoia dragging behind me like an anchor. What the fuck was I doing there?

I remember seeing Le Tissier waving to us from the back of the club minibus as we made that long run down Hill Lane. The minibus carried the Lucozade drinks that were brought up for us when we arrived at the sports centre car park, the halfway point, and he'd got a lift back in it. That's not a story to embellish his famously lethargic attitude to physical exercise. Le Tissier *hated* the running part of pre-season training but he was forgiven because . . . well, because he was a genius.

Back then, pre-season training involved a lot of running. After a week of running around the common, the sports centre and the muni golf course in Southampton, we got on a coach that took us to an army camp near Littleton in Winchester. The warm-up was a four-mile run around the camp followed by an hour of water aerobics. The laughter and wisecracks soon subsided when half of the squad almost drowned. I'd be rubbish in the army. I'm an inherent coward at the best of times but being told, or should I say shouted at, to 'fucking grow some balls!' while cramping up in every fibre of my body made the thrill of wearing a pair of official Southampton training shorts in a swimming pool in Winchester feel worse than hell. And that was on the first session of the first day there. The funny thing was I kept bobbing my head above the waterline. Not too often, but often enough to stay alive in this most thrilling but intimidating of atmospheres.

The balls came out in the afternoons and every now and then I'd do something decent. Not the sort of relentless, quality demonstrations laid on by a proper footballer – Matthew Le Tissier, for example – but the sort of stupid stuff that frustratingly suggested I was far better than I actually was; levels that were enough to suggest I was reluctant to reveal a hidden gem of very rare class given time and patience.

I got quite pally with Paul Allen for a couple of days (back in 1980, Allen set a record as the youngest FA Cup winner, at 17 years and 256 days old), primarily due to the fact that we'd shared the top and tail endeavours of carrying a twelve-foot timber log on our shoulders across the army range on the Tuesday morning. Although I was training with the reserves in the afternoon football session, the first team were seldom far away. They were having a drinks break and were watching on when I received a ball with my back to goal. I can't remember how it happened, but I turned the defender marking me and smashed it into the top corner of the net from all of 25 yards. Then we had our drinks break.

'Some strike that, big man!' said Paul Allen. (*Paul Allen said that!*)

'I don't know what happened there,' I replied sheepishly. The trouble was, I meant it. I was as astounded as anyone that I could do such a thing. In fact, I spent the majority of the seven weeks I spent with Southampton trying not to do anything right. Or good. I spent 95 per cent of my time there trying not to fuck things up and look like a cunt. That's not a great mindset. I remember speaking to the old man on a weekly basis.

'Just go and enjoy it,' he'd say. 'It doesn't matter, you've got to believe you're as good as them otherwise there's no point. Enjoy it and take 'em on. Don't pass the fuckin' thing all the time. If you do what they say, you'll end up ordinary.'

I dreamt of being ordinary in that sort of company, and I'm not even talking about the first teamers.

In one training session, I remember being given the task of providing flick-ons at the near post from corners. It's not a tricky skill to pull off, the flick-on. All that's required is to make minimal contact with the ball as it comes into the box and deflect it towards the back post for an incoming teammate to put it in the net. I'd almost made minimal contact a trademark in front of goal when we were attacking, anyway, so I can understand the reserve team manager Dave Merrington's thinking by getting me out of the way in front of the near post. He understandably thought that we'd be a lot more effective that way. Trouble was, I suddenly became proficient at making full-blooded contact with every corner that came in. This was an unopposed session, *no defenders*, and I was now heading the ball vast distances away from the area into which I was supposed to flick it into while under no pressure whatsoever.

Paradoxically, I was told to defend the near post when we were defending corners and all I seemed to do was perform the most dangerous flick-ons imaginable across our own goalmouth instead. Again, *all* of this was unopposed.

I was so nervous and so rigid with the fear of failure that anything I was easily capable of became something I was utterly *incapable* of. I was fully aware of this problem, but suffered from some sort of schizophrenic disorder. One part of me was a rational ally; the other was the ultimate rug-puller.

'*You can do this, Michael.*'

'Yeah, but just imagine if you don't. You'd look a right twat if you fucked it up. Don't fuck it up.'

'*You can't fuck this up, surely?*'

'I rather think you can, just try to keep your eye on the ball. Remember, this is a training session without any opposition. Whatever you do, don't make full contact. If you do that, you might end up doing it over and over and over again, with the real professionals thinking you're a fucking idiot.'

THUD.

'Fuck.'

'*You're an idiot.*'

'I know I am.'

'*You surely can't do that again, can you?*'

THUD.

'Fuck!'

'*You're starting to look like a proper cunt.*'

I'm not exaggerating when I say that it became a debilitating psychological nightmare.

So why was I even there? It all seems so ludicrous as I sit here today, writing down memories that I both treasure yet simultaneously shudder with shame to recall.

The simple reason was Alan Ball.

I'd been to plenty of clubs that he'd been at as a manager. I was on schoolboy forms when he was at Portsmouth and I played in his youth team at Exeter during holidays and half-term when I was doing my A levels in Winchester. I was sort of his mascot, I suppose, and Alan was always a source of encouragement. I wouldn't say he was 'a fan' of mine, but he did everything to get the best out of me. He was brilliant at that, encouraging young people, inspiring people whom he believed in. It seems strange that he fell out with so many of the established professionals he managed in football, because with youngsters he was as good as anyone I could imagine.

But there was always the anvil around my neck.

It was always there; the feeling of associated nepotism, what with Bally being Mick's best mate. That was the single debilitating effect on my psyche. I felt incapable, incompetent and unworthy most of the time – and utterly paranoid for all of it. Alan's son Jimmy was at the Dell at the same time, and we were total opposites. Jimmy would front up to anyone, speak when he wasn't spoken to and give as good as he got. And then some. I suppose things reached their nadir when the local press got hold of the story that both Jimmy and I were training with Saints during pre-season. 'CHANNON & BALL PART 2!' screamed the headlines. Oh shit.

While Jimmy said that he was determined to do everything within his powers to make it as a footballer, I remember saying that I was going to go to university to become a journalist. I thought that would do as a cover story because I was signing on at the time and had very little idea of what I wanted to actually do apart from football. I just didn't want to say that I wanted to be a footballer. That would have made me look silly in the face of what I knew was going to end in failure.

A terrifically positive outlook from someone who had been given the opportunity to do the only thing he'd ever wanted, at the only club he'd ever wanted to do it at. They even took photographs of the two of us together in our training kit at Wellington Sports Ground. They got me to sit on the groundsman's tractor for one of them, and I remember thinking that was the best place for me. I knew how to drive a tractor.

I hated it. Grandma Avril kept all of the cuttings from the *Daily Echo*. Even worse, we made the *Mirror* a few days later.

An established pro called Perry Groves was training with the reserves at the time. He'd been a decent player for a quality Arsenal side before he came to Saints, but he'd snapped his Achilles tendon very early on after his arrival and was trying to regain his fitness and form. He was very gobby, but equally as likeable, and never let you off with anything. He drove into training every day from his home in Hertfordshire, and I'll never forget the moment I drove my Volvo 340 into the iron gates at the Dell. That moment still visits me in my sleep. Inevitably, Perry Groves was getting out of his car when it happened. He slaughtered me and made sure the rest of the squad heard about it.

I ought to make you aware of the fact that it was a Sunday morning and I was very hung over. By this time, with the Premier League season beckoning, I was almost pleading for this footballing purgatory to end, as I rubbed shoulders with some of my heroes while continuing to play like I had a physical disability. Quite frankly, if I wasn't *actually* an embarrassment to others, I was embarrassed for myself. As a result, I went on the piss the Saturday prior to my collision with the Dell gates to numb the worry of another day ahead. I had been bladdered that Saturday night. Consequently, I was very hot and very sweaty as I shivered my way down Hill Lane before turning left onto Milton Road and turning the immediate left yet again into the car park at the Dell on that balmy, late summer morning. I went to swing the 340 the immediate 90 degrees into the car park, but halfway through this manoeuvre the steering wheel slipped through my sweaty palms, straightened up and I crunched into the iron gate at about 20 miles an hour.

As a motor car, the Volvo 340 was a notoriously solid and sturdy model, and the noise of the collision matched the ferocity of the impact. As I scraped the 340 Volvo into a parking space in front of the old ground, with the bumper gouging a furrow into the tarmac, Perry Groves's face greeted me. His laughter echoed in my ears and grew louder and louder as I sheepishly got out and walked over to the iron gate to fetch the remnants of the headlamp, which had shattered into small but annoyingly retrievable pieces. It was one of those Volvo 340 headlamps with a mini-windscreen wiper attached to it.

We were training on the pitch at the Dell that morning so I had to endure Perry's retelling of the incident as we got changed. Some of the lads even went out to look and they, in turn, fetched even more of the lads out before everyone on Southampton's groundstaff was reduced into similar hysterics.

I then went on to block a shot from Jason Dodd in the training session and caught it right in the bollocks.

'Not your day is it, son?' cackled Perry Groves.

The howls of laughter . . . I can still hear them. That sort of sums up my time at the Dell.

As does hitting the bar against Bognor Regis in a pre-season friendly. A cross came over and it was perfect, all I had to do was get my head on it and it would go in. The only major problem I had was that I knew it was perfect and that all I had to do was get my head on it and it would go in. I was so fraught with the consequences of missing yet so keen to do well that it was physically impossible to do so. And I mean, *physically impossible*. I was so tense that hitting the bar unchallenged from three yards out felt like success. It was that good a cross that heading it over was almost impossible.

Breaking David Hughes's leg is another moment I remember of that game. Hughesie was a very talented player who'd had more than his fair share of injuries, so expecting me to return his throw-in was the last thing he wanted to do at that stage of his ultimately unfulfilled career. I didn't actually break his leg myself but I was certainly the architect of it because the physical act of side-footing a volley back to him was so far beyond my capabilities that a long spell in plaster was the least he should have expected when I dropped the return short and a non-league full-back hit him halfway up his fibula.

That's played on my mind for ages.

So many embarrassing moments haunt me still.

Circuit training at the Dell, for instance. There was a small multi-gym down by the tunnel in the corner of the ground, and the entire reserve team squad would cram in there once a week. The pacesetter was always the bloke doing chin-ups, and in the time he did ten chin-ups the rest of us had to do as many squat thrusts, burpees, sit-ups, press-ups, etc., in that period. The sooner the guy on chin-ups did his ten, the easier it was on the rest of the lads. Chin-ups are really, really hard by the way.

Halfway through that first session, it came to be my turn to set the pace on the chin-up bars. I wasn't fully grown but I was six feet four inches by then, yet built like a jockey's whip. I could only manage four.

FOUR!

If I'm honest, if I hadn't have been embarrassingly relieved of the responsibility by Dave Merrington, the entire reserve team would still be in that little room today.

And they knocked the Dell down in 2001.

I'm squirming at the memory.

Throughout all this, I was trying *so* hard that the effort became counterproductive. If you want *anything* in life too much: a pay-rise, a girl, a contract from Southampton Football Club, then the process of pursuing it becomes mentally draining, technically impossible and ultimately futile.

I kept my insecurities and paranoia to myself. Humiliation leads you towards adopting an insular mentality and you never imagine that anyone can see that struggle. Least of all a man who is old enough to be your grandad.

I was sitting in the waiting room of my dentist at the top of Hill Lane, as you do. The door opened from the dentist's room and as I was called in I noticed that the person leaving was Ted Bates, 'Mr Southampton' himself. He was club president by then, Mick's first manager, a club legend, and a great man. He *was* like your grandad.

'Hello, Michael.'

'Hello, Ted . . . Mr Bates . . . Ted—'

'How's everything going?'

'Good, thanks. Good,' I lied.

'How's your dad?'

'Good, thanks.'

'How's your mum? You live with her, don't you? At the top of The Avenue.'

'Yes, Ted, by Stoneham Golf Club.'

Ted knew everything about everyone who was connected to Southampton Football Club. It was his life. 'Good lad. Give her my love, won't you?'

'I will, Ted. Mr Bates . . .' I made my way towards the dentist's room.

'Oh, Michael . . .'

I looked back.

'. . . *You're trying too hard.*' Ted Bates smiled kindly, walked out of the door and onto Hill Lane. I went in and had a filling.

I wasn't aware he even knew I was at the Dell, let alone that he'd been watching me.

That was the first crumb of comfort I'd had since I'd been there. Nothing specific, nothing to do with football, just an observation that made me feel slightly less of an idiot. I don't think for one minute that Ted Bates thought I was good enough to be a footballer, but he could see the symptoms I was suffering from at that time, and he made me feel better about myself as a person. I can still see him standing by the door of the dentist on Hill Lane now: very unassuming, very kind, a jacket and a tie, a sympathetic smile on his face.

'Oh, Michael . . . You're trying too hard.'

I understand what his ex-players mean when they talk of his man management. He was a truly great man. Bollocks to football. *That* was a moment that meant something to someone other than an aspiring footballer.

Things got better from then on in. The first team left for a tour of Scandinavia and Dave Merrington went with them. That meant that Bally and the reserve team manager who had seen my early efforts and awful performances were out of the picture. That suited me down to the ground and, for a brief period, I ceased being an embarrassment and started smiling a lot more. Grumbling professionals frustrated at being left behind and superb professionals determined to make a statement rattled around the now half-full training ground along with the apprentices and a handful of triallists. It was a strange mix of attitudes, ages and expectancy. I started to play half decent. Not *well*, but half decent, and I started to enjoy it for a brief period. I remember a young lad called Frankie Bennett scoring a hat-trick one evening against a non-league side. I don't remember the opposition. He was electric, Frankie Bennett: not much of a footballer but very quick and a real handful up front. Alongside me. I did well that night. I set up most of the goals and wasn't embarrassed when a young Saints fan asked for my autograph at the final whistle. I did all right and I liked myself a little. That was great, as good as I could do. I was one of the better ones that night.

The first team returned ten days before the Premier League was due to start (away at Newcastle) and on the Monday morning they lined up against the reserves for what Bally wanted to be played as 'a proper game'. Some full of bitterness, some full of ambition, the reserves ripped into the first team and went two up inside ten minutes. I was playing up front with a lad called Colin Cramb. If truth be told, this was a genuine mismatch. The reserves had nothing to lose and plenty to prove, while none of the first team wanted to get injured as the end of a hard pre-season approached and the season proper beckoned. We were battering them.

An angry Bally intervened – he could do that whistle by putting his fingers in his mouth. He then went mental. Adopt the high-pitched Lancashire accent again: 'If you don't want to play football you can fuck off and do something else for a living! I've never in my life seen such a pathetic display from professional footballers! Start passing it, start demanding it, start playing! Right! For the next ten minutes, every fourth pass has to go to Le Tissier!'

I don't think I can do justice to what happened next. Le Tissier, lethargic and uninterested up until then, came alive. He knew he was going to get the ball, and I've never seen such quality. It was stupid, really, because, for a brief period, he seemed to be everywhere. I don't think he'd covered that much ground in the previous six weeks of pre-season. He got the ball, he beat a man, he passed it. He passed it and passed it and passed it. My abiding memory is of him standing by the corner flag as Cramb and I rushed in. He collected the ball from Dave Beasant, the keeper, and chipped it up with his back to goal as I arrived on the scene.

He just shouted, 'Jeff!' I can still hear it fizzing past my left ear as he volleyed it fully 40 yards and it landed on Jeff Kenna's chest, in the full-back position on the other side of the pitch. He jogged off to get involved again with Bally's praise echoing around the training ground. It was quite a thing to see. I'll never forget it or the impression it made on me. I'm not overstating the fact; he had greatness in him. An astonishing talent.

I was in the shower afterwards – they have good showers at professional football clubs – and having run around like a nutter for the best part of an hour, trying to make up for the talent I lacked, I was in no hurry to leave. I was knackered.

In walks Matt Le Tissier.

'All right, Michael?'

'Yeah.'

We had some sort of a conversation, but I can't remember what we said because I was somewhere else, thinking about what I'd just seen. He was *that* good that *I* felt good. He was that good that I didn't feel under pressure any more. There's no shame in not being good enough to be a professional footballer, certainly when the difference between being half decent and a top professional is an immeasurable chasm. Sure, I'd wasted an opportunity to do myself justice through my lack of mental strength and the pressure I'd heaped upon myself because of who my dad was, but it was OK now. Perhaps my paranoia was exactly that? Perhaps not everyone resented me. Perhaps I *wasn't* that bad anyway. I'd had a go. Not many people have that opportunity and, for all my embarrassment, I'm glad I experienced it.

If nothing else, to witness Le Tissier's performance on that Monday morning was amazing. I've watched him score goals before and after that day as a supporter, but for twenty minutes he probably didn't get any better in my opinion. I'm not lying either.

His manager inspired him.

His manager loved him.

Le Tissier wasn't the best player at the club. That sounds like a daft statement, but he wasn't. The best player at the club would have the first pick of three players for five-a-sides in the cavernous gym at the Dell every Friday afternoon. He wouldn't move any further than three yards and he didn't have to. He probably couldn't either because he was 49 years of age.

Alan Ball ran me ragged one afternoon. I can't explain what he did but he never took more than one touch and knew exactly what I was going to do. He'd anticipate where to be for the return pass because he knew what I'd do before he'd even set the ball in motion in the first place. He made me move where he wanted me to go so he didn't have to work his gammy knee. He had me running round in circles. He was incredible – easily the most intelligent footballer I can imagine there ever being. I'm sure others would say the same. Unbelievable.

He had won the World Cup though. There's no shame in that, is there?

After that Monday session when Le Tissier provided perspective, I was told to report to the Dell to see the boss in his office. The team's photo-call was on the Monday afternoon and the reserves had their first league game against Millwall on Tuesday evening. I was slightly confused by all of this because it all seemed a bit formal – being asked to see Bally in his office. That said, I had done quite well in the last few weeks. Inside my head, the rational ally and the rug-puller returned:

'You did lay on a hat-trick for Frankie Bennett the other night . . .'

'Don't be so daft, you broke Hughesie's leg, you couldn't score against Bognor Regis and you drove the Volvo 340 into the gates at the Dell.'

I didn't even know where Bally's office was. As it turned out, it was up the iron staircase in a room next to what used to be the players' lounge above the club shop. Twelve years earlier, my sister Nicky and I would watch *The Pink Panther* and *The Dukes of Hazzard* on the telly after home games in that room, when the old man was playing and ruled the roost. I wasn't my old man, although I knew his best mate.

In an adjacent room to the old lounge I turned a corner and there was Bally sitting at his desk, the door propped open by a fire extinguisher. I remembered what he'd said on that first morning of pre-season training: *'My door is always open!'*

I sheepishly knocked, a part of me wondering if my improved level of form since the first team's disappearance to Scandinavia had got back to the manager. Was I worth another month? The team photo is this afternoon, is that why I'm here? To be a Saints player, in the famous eve-of-season club photo?

Adopt that high-pitched Lancashire accent again:

'Come on in, son . . . *Shut the door.*' I cast my mind back to Alan's brief speech on the first day of pre-season when we were all gathered in the car park prior to running round the sport centre. He said then that his door was *always* open.

Oh, bollocks.

The game was up, so I grinned. Alan didn't. I pulled the fire extinguisher across the tiled carpet and the door shut courtesy of the spring-loaded hinge. I sat down as I was asked to but, to be honest, there really was no need for us to go through the professional courtesies. I was still grinning nervously and self-consciously but Alan gave me time, spoke to me with respect and thanked me for all the effort I'd put in. Granted, it was weird and, yes, I couldn't wait for it to end, but I love him for that. He treated me like a man that day.

'You've done well. I know how hard you've found it physically, you're six foot four and less than fourteen stone. You're very hard on yourself at times but you've done all you can.' Dave Merrington even joined us halfway through and chipped in with his own brand of positive feedback. This was above and beyond what I needed, and I couldn't wait to get back to being as we were before this whole football stuff got in the way. He'd been 'the boss' for seven long weeks now and I wanted to get back to Sunday lunch with him in Hursley and a laugh at Goodwood races. Just the two of us. And my dad.

'Have you picked up your expenses?' he asked.

That was confusing. 'Expenses?'

'For your travel, your lunches. Are we all square?'

'Erm, I didn't think that was part of the thing.'

'Seven weeks, I make it. We'll call it eight. Go and see Carol at reception.'

We shook hands and I wandered down the iron staircase and across the forecourt to the main office. Inside ten minutes I was given an envelope. I remember fetching my boots from the boot room at the Dell. They were Puma Kings. I even had an apprentice, believe it or not, who was responsible for laying my kit out and polishing my boots every day I was there. His name was Matthew Oakley (FA Cup finalist in 2003, Arsenal 1 Southampton 0). A super lad.

Anyway, I got into the Volvo 340, opened the envelope that Carol had given me in the office and counted out £800. That was over a hundred quid a week for my time on trial at Southampton Football Club. Certainly not performance-related pay, but more than Matthew Oakley was on at that time, and definitely enough to cover the cost of the new bumper and a headlamp with a mini-windscreen wiper attached to it. I suppose that sort of made me a professional footballer.

Sort of.

It was a relief, in truth. I was very close to Bally but it's hard to please a father figure who has achieved so much in the same professional capacity. To them it seems so easy.

So, in the late summer of 1994, that was me done. I was far from prepared but I had a girlfriend who channelled my mind into moving in a different direction if things didn't turn out as I wished. Thickos got into university through a process called 'clearing' back then and a place at the University of the West of England had been secured for that autumn.

Bristol beckoned.

A place that I enjoyed immensely.

Colliding with a patio the following May wasn't the best thing I could have done but I honestly think things turned out well.

Eventually.

I've written this, after all. Mum can always sell it in the shop . . .

SECONDITIS

WEDNESDAY 24 JUNE 2015

All you can do is try. That's what I've learnt. If you put the effort in, regardless of your talent, things will go right in the end. Or so I keep telling myself anyway.

Today was another one of frustration, but there are signs that we're not far away from getting things right. More importantly, I made a trip to Winchester ahead of an afternoon at Salisbury races before a meeting at Bath this evening. It's my mum Jane's birthday today. She's great, my mum. Having worked in the pub trade in the north-west for ten years or so, my sister Nicky and I eventually convinced her to 'retire' and come back south where she'd be closer to her grandkids. She moved back but retirement was never going to be embraced for too long. She's a hard worker is mum, always has been. About seven or eight years ago she decided to do a few hours part time for Wessex Cancer Trust and we all knew it wouldn't ever be part time. Within six weeks she was full time and managing the shop in Weeke, just outside Winchester, and it's now one of the most successful charity shops in the country.

I headed to Winchester before Salisbury today and earned 'son of the year' status by popping into the Waitrose next door to mum's shop to buy her some flowers. There's excellent parking

Mum and the girls in the shop

facilities, so I allied an air of generosity with very convenient logistics to look like a very loving young man. I ought to counter this by saying that these charity shops are excellent value and I picked up Peter Kay's autobiography and a best of Crowded House CD for less than four quid. I gave them a tenner just to throw them off the scent that I was the real winner in the whole escapade.

By the way, have you any idea of what those meerkat toys – the ones from the insurance company – go for? Mum says they put them in the window at twenty quid and they are snapped up inside an hour. If you have one, give it to a charity shop, they are one of the biggest earners going, Mum says, and she should know. She virtually *lives* there.

Salisbury this afternoon saw Unilit finish second in a two-year-old conditions race later in the day – a pleasing showing for a filly who had won her maiden at Pontefract three weeks ago.

A syndicate, Insignia Racing, owns her, and they are a fun bunch to train for.

Likewise, Jersey Brown finished second in the opener under Danny Cremin at Bath this evening. She too has a smashing owner in Sue Bunney. Lovely owners make the job so easy – if only the opposition wasn't around to continue a run of second places and make it so hard.

We're doing OK, though, it'll come right soon – it has to – you can't keep working like we do without having your turn in the spotlight.

THE JOHN RADCLIFFE VOMITING JAMBOREE

TUESDAY 7 – WEDNESDAY 8 JULY 2015

A strange and scary day. The usual beginning: a 5.30 a.m. start, a cup of tea and over to the indoor ride to trot the first lot ahead of their exercise. We're starting early at the moment due to the heatwave that everyone seems to be moaning about. (I'm not sure why, because it'll soon be piss wet and miserably cold again.) We're basically doing as much as the weather will permit us at the moment, and even though Tuesdays, along with Fridays, are our work mornings, the ground is so firm that we're restricted to the six-furlong all-weather gallop at present. That's always a worry because all of our fast work takes place on the grass, and although the horses are a picture of health, results suggest otherwise. When you have a run like we're having, a million different thoughts cross your mind. You're always questioning the process.

No great shakes, with all the horses taken care of after fourth lot, before Mick and I went for a bit of lunch with our friends and owners Peter Taplin and Sue Bunney at midday. I then went home for a kip in the afternoon before driving Paddy Pilley to Brighton where we had two runners that evening.

Paddy is very much the flavour of the month at present and is riding plenty of winners – although, to be honest, his ride on Knight Of The Air in the third race left a lot to be desired. He looked all over the shop and resembled a string of spaghetti rather than a professional jockey of the future, coming second in a pretty untidy finish.

He made amends half an hour later though and brought home Juventas for her second win in a week. I phoned the old man back at home.

'Hello.' His voice seemed a bit shaky but I cracked on.

'All right. Did you see that Knight Of The Air ride?'

'Yeah, it wasn't the best – a typical kid's ride.'

'Yeah, exactly. That was all right, though, at least the filly's a racehorse again.'

'Yeah.' He didn't have any emotion about him and, for once, I was driving the conversation. As I was processing this he came back with, 'I'm not well, Michael. I'll speak in the morning,' and just put the phone down.

Now, we're all entitled to be ill now and again, but it was the way that he admitted it and called me Michael that stuck in my mind on the drive home. I got in at about half-ten, had a beer and went to bed. I couldn't sleep, though.

At about half-one in the morning my phone, which I usually keep on silent mode, lit up with a voicemail message. Terror began to rise, because there was a missed call from the old man as well. I dialled voicemail and listened to a strange voice on the other end of the line, 'Michael, I'm in bits. I've called for the ambulance. Get here quick.'

T-shirt, shorts and trainers on, I legged it to the big house about two hundred yards from where I live in the yard. A grey, very sweaty man was slumped in the kitchen in his pyjamas. It was Mick.

'I've been throwing up for two hours. I don't know what it is, but I'm in bits. It was like black, brown soil.'

He looked awful. 'How long have you been like this?'

'Since about eight o'clock this morning.' I became less concerned and angrier. Very angry, in fact. He never shows weakness and never expresses his feelings, apart from his anger (or 'frustration' as he famously calls it), and now here he is, facing his biggest fear in life: relying on the assistance of others.

A car pulled up outside the house, one of those paramedic estates, and a cheery woman came to the door, bringing the usual cumbersome kit with her into the kitchen.

'Hello, my name is Judy. What's your name?'

'Michael Channon,' said the old man.

Michael Channon? What the fuck is going on here?

I just sat to one side next to the kitchen table, trying not to get in the way or talk for the old man. Despite the pain he was in and the depth of concern etched on his face, he'd have hated me to intervene. He was still trying to hold it together. He explained the events of the day: he'd felt dreadful since eight in the morning and only had the bowl of soup in the Swan pub with Pete, Sue and myself at midday. My anger again began to rise. Why doesn't he just say he's not well?

Judy began to wire him up to one of those machines that go 'ping', took his blood pressure and told us that she used to come over to the stables to play with all the staff's children that lived on site during her childhood. Mick mentioned something about Nashwan, a good guess I thought considering her age. Nashwan won the Derby when he was trained here in 1989 and Judy would be late thirties probably, certainly no older than me, and here she was, assessing my old man, who was in such a state that he was allowing somebody else to help him.

My concern began to ease now that Judy was there, until Mick went white as a sheet and began to sweat profusely. His light blue T-shirt turned dark very quickly and he gestured towards the sink tub he had by his feet. I grabbed it and put it on his lap.

Now, I've seen vomit before, and I'm no stranger to the act myself, but this was a cut above the norm. This was truly world-class vomiting, like something out of *Family Guy*. What was even more alarming was the fact that it was a browny-black colour, as if he'd been on a twelve-hour bender of Bovril and topsoil. Judy was unflappable in the face of what, to me, was a shocking yet hugely impressive insight into what the human body can both achieve and produce.

I decided to throw caution to the wind and ask what anyone would want to know in such a situation. 'He's not going to cark it, is he?' This question prompted the old man to try to utter what I think was, 'Fuck off,' although it was hard to tell because he was still retching, groaning and spitting into the sink tub.

'I'm sure he'll be fine, but he will be going for a trip in the ambulance,' said Judy.

'So he's definitely not going to cark it?' I asked for reassurance.

Mick was now bright red and looking at me as if I'd forgotten he was even in the room, which to all intents and purposes I had. It was a question he'd have wanted to know anyway, so I thought I'd take the bull by the horns.

'The ambulance is on the way; what's the best place to go from here?'

'Well, the John Radcliffe is the best one around. They've got everything covered, haven't they?' I said, not entirely convinced that this was the routine case that Judy was implying it was. To my mind, it was best to make sure he went to the big place in Oxford. From my limited knowledge of hospitals and medical care, bigger was always better, and Oxford's 'JR' dwarfed the one in nearby Thatcham.

She turned to the old man. 'Michael,' (*Michael! I still couldn't believe my ears*) 'on a scale of one to ten, how much pain are you in?'

'Eight,' he replied, gesturing at me with the half-full sink bowl. I took it and rinsed it down the sink. '*Eight.*' Now that was pretty bad. For Mick to admit to that much pain, he was truly in a terrible way. He's been suffering from arthritis since he stopped playing football. The bones in his hands and feet have fused together as a result and it doesn't take a genius to work out that this constant pain plays a major part in both his mood and demeanour.

By my own pathetic numerical assessment he must have played well over 900 games as a professional footballer and you can double that effort in terms of training, friendlies and exhibition matches through his twenty years as an athlete. The 1970s miracle drug called cortisone meant that he played a quarter of those games through local anaesthetic, so that probably played its part in not only his longevity as an athlete but also his trust in prescription drugs.

'Are you on medication, Michael?' asked Judy, as Mick's pain-filled face tried to think of detail.

'No. Not for anything serious.'

'Have you suffered from any heart troubles in recent years?'

'No, none at all.'

'So you don't have any allergies or health issues?' Judy looked at me for confirmation.

I confirmed that he was, for his age, a completely healthy 66-year-old man. And he is. Two of his best mates, Bally and Peter Osgood died young through heart attacks, so he's been more aware than anyone of the need to prevent risking another similar sudden checkout. Through genetics, not design, he's A1. If there was any family trait of heart disease I know he'd have been stone dead a long time ago. Grandad Jack snuffed it at the age of 84, but that was after 59 years of Grandma's cooking, and she's still living in her bungalow in the stable yard at the age of 93. She's a country girl, is Grandma, and gravy had been the staple diet of Grandad Jack (indeed all of us).

The week before he died Bally told me that he had a bike, and we had all the tools at our disposal to ensure that 'the angry bastard won't have a heart attack'. He was moving into the next door village of East Ilsley, and he saw his relocation to a more central part of the country as a means to not only ease his own time on the road as an after-dinner speaker but also to be closer to his best mate. The Sunday barbeques with his neighbour and best friend that we spoke about and looked forward to with such enthusiasm were dashed three days later, and Mick was left to do nothing other than ensure his cardiovascular health was tip-top as a result. Mick probably still dwells on a loss that I suspect he feels on an almost daily basis, but he only refers to Bally's sudden death as a lesson in life – with a swear word towards fate thrown in for good measure.

Back in the kitchen, Judy was asking him if he'd ever been administered morphine.

'Yeah! I could do with some of that. I love it.'

'What are these scars on your arm, Michael?'

'I got smashed up in a car crash a few years back, that's why I know about morphine.' Judy looked at me again for confirmation.

'He's had morphine before,' I said. 'No allergies, no medical issues apart from that,' I nodded. Judy gave him the morphine and some anti-sickness drugs as we waited for the ambulance to arrive.

I scurried over to the house to put on some jeans and grab a top. I was told to bring something for him to read because he'd be in hospital for quite some time. I knew that he had some books that would interest him in the office, but in my panic I couldn't find the keys so I brought him two books that I had in my downstairs toilet.

As I returned to the kitchen his eyes fixed on me immediately. He'd been sick on his T-shirt and he wanted me to fetch another. I did so, but by the time I returned the ambulance crew had seen that he'd been sick. Despite the pain and the worry I could see the shame he felt. I felt proud but incredibly sad at exactly the same time. *Does this bloke think he's immortal?* I reckon he does, which both scares and inspires me. 'Right, I've got two books for you. One is an academic study of the Wehrmacht and the Nazis, the other is on the Busby Babes and their legacy after the Munich air crash.'

'I'll read the one about Hitler,' he mumbled as they helped him to his feet.

'I bet you fucking will!' I said. 'But it's a text book, meaning there aren't any pictures in it, so I'll bring the Busby Babes along.' He looked disappointed. (*That actually happened.*)

As I followed the ambulance up the A34 I began to panic. I'd been in this position before but now I was seriously worried about the consequences of Mick dying. The emotional part of dealing with his loss I'm almost prepared for, but now I adopted a far more sober outlook on what his snuffing it would mean to the business and ultimately me. I feel ashamed of that, but that was what went through my mind. We are in no position to ever move on without the old man running the show. Thoughts and scenarios raced through my mind. What owners would want me to train their horses? How many orders for yearlings are people going to place with me in charge? We'd have to sell the yard. We'd have to lay off the staff. If we did that, I'd have liquefied his hard-earned legacy in just a couple of months. I'm useless, redundant and pointless. Everyone would know it as well. Such thoughts often roost in my mind, even when I'm not following my dad in an ambulance at four o'clock in the morning, but this time they were brought even more sharply into focus.

Fuck.

We got to the Accident & Emergency department at the John Radcliffe. I parked the car up and scurried over to the ambulance as Mick was being brought out of the back. John, the paramedic who travelled with him in the back, and the tattooed driver, whose name I forget, were easing him down the mechanical ramp. What a state. There was vomit everywhere. John was saying, 'I've not seen a performance like that in the back for quite some time!' – all delivered in a very matter-of-fact tone, while I tried to register the sheer volume of fluid before me. It truly must have been quite a 'performance'. It was even on the ceiling.

They wheeled him in and he asked me if I had yet another clean T-shirt. I did. In the curtained assessment cubicle a doctor joined us; top bloke, very calm, utterly reassuring.

'Hello, I'm Tim, can you tell me your full name and your date of birth?' Mick was getting very good at this process by now, although he kept gesturing to me about a fresh T-shirt. Tim would be back shortly after they'd taken some blood and hooked him up to a drip and another, bigger machine that goes 'ping'.

As I sat there watching two nurses either side of Mick, one taking blood from his right arm and the other attaching the blood pressure sleeve to his left, the tattooed ambulance driver reappeared. Ten minutes had passed and Mick was looking worse than ever by now and shaking quite remarkably.

'I've just realised who you are!' said the ambulance driver.

The two girls attending to Mick looked at the driver, then back at Mick, and then back at the driver. They would have been in their mid-twenties, tops, and were clearly confused. 'Err, who is he, then?' said the girl who was trying in vain to find a vein.

'I used to play soccer,' mumbled Mick, clearly trying to act chipper but looking more unlike any professional footballer ever had.

'Did you?' said the doubtful nurse on his other arm.

'Yeah,' said Mick.

Nobody knew what to say, least of all the nurses. Thankfully, the tattooed driver chipped in: 'I just hope that they make you more comfortable and wish you all the best.'

'Thank you very much, thanks for everything,' slurred Mick.

The ambulance driver turned on his heels and left. It wasn't going to play out in the manner that I suspected, after all.

Ten minutes later John, who had clearly made short work of cleaning up the back of the ambulance, also appeared in the cubicle. Mick's left arm was now being hooked up to a drip, although the nurse trying to take blood out of his right arm was still toiling away. 'I've just been told who you are! It didn't register at first but I suppose we had other things to concern us!' he said warmly.

'That's all right. Bloody hell, you must have a long memory,' slurred Mick as John turned to an administration table a few feet away and grabbed a sheet of paper.

'I was wondering . . . could you sign this for my next-door neighbour? She's 91 and a massive Southampton supporter.'

I sat there, open-mouthed as Mick with a drip in one arm and a needle in the other, and shaking like a leaf, accepted the paper and a pen from John and failed to hold either with any form of control.

'Her name's Ida.'

'How do you spell that?'

'I-D-A,' said John.

Mick somehow managed to make contact between the two items in his hands and made an effort to not only spell 'Ida' but his own name as well. John offered his thanks and his best wishes and made his exit as we all looked at each other.

'Well, you never know, that might have been a smart move,' I said.

'Why?' was all Mick could say.

'Because the last autograph John Lennon signed is worth a fortune, although he didn't dedicate it to someone called Ida, and people called Ida are a bit thin on the ground these days.'

It was now the turn of the nurses and Mick to look at me with confusion and bemusement.

(That actually happened.)

When the situation returned to something approaching normal, Mick was given some anti-sickness medication and morphine, which allowed him to sleep for a couple of hours as the drip rehydrated him, and I settled down to read about the Busby Babes. By the time the famous Manchester United team had been beaten in the FA Cup final of 1957 (Aston Villa won 2–1) it was half-past six in the morning, Mick had had an hour's kip and Tim was back with the results of the blood tests: 'We've found nothing, I'm afraid. It's all come back clear, and I can see from your physical appearance that you're not a heavy drinker, you don't smoke and, aside from a few incidents in the past, you're as healthy as can be expected.'

'That's right, yes.' said the old man. Colour had returned to his face and he looked like he usually does. A bit grumpy but otherwise fine.

'Right,' continued Tim. 'As far as I can tell, you've suffered some form of a stomach bleed, probably caused by an ulcer. This isn't uncommon and would explain the grainy, coffee-coloured vomiting you've endured. It's far from unusual but we will probably have to keep you in until we can perform an endoscopy to have a look and see what the root of the trouble is. I'll be back in a minute or two.'

Mick didn't like this news. 'If anyone hears I'm in here they'll think I've had a fucking heart attack and think that I'm dying, or something. With the way the horses are running they'll desert us like rats from a sinking ship.'

'I know, Dad, but we've got to let them do what they've got to do.'

'What time is it?'

'Nearly seven.'

'What about the entries and decs?'

'I've already got a *Racing Post* and there's Wi-Fi in here so we'll sort it while we wait.'

'Is Ross in the office? What have you told them?'

'Just that we're in here because you were throwing up all night.'

'You haven't told them anything else, have you?'

'Like what? Like you've had a heart attack and you're dying, or something?'

'Good. Right, I don't think we can run that Volunteer Point because we haven't had the rain that was forecast . . .'

We just cracked on as if nothing had happened. I texted it all through to our racing secretary, Ross Potter, and the entries and declarations for our runners were made. Not exactly textbook placing of our horses but sometimes needs must. That's how Mick is. Work has and always will be at the forefront of his mind.

Having been kept up to date, Ross ensured that we were as on top of things as we possibly could be, so I phoned the only person I could at a time like this. Mick's Jill was away on holiday, so I called Nicky.

'Right, don't worry, but I'm in the John Radcliffe with Dad. He's OK, but will be in here for a bit longer, and I've not slept all night. Can you help me out?'

My sister is one of those unflappable individuals who can normally get things done despite juggling three kids around between school and their sporting activities. She shuffled the kids around and made the trip up from her home just outside of Winchester to be in the JR by 12.45 to relieve me of my duties. She cheerily agreed to keep Mick up to date with three mares that he had going through the sales ring at Tattersalls in Newmarket that afternoon, and I set off for home.

Endoscopies need to be fitted in when it suits the NHS, not when it suits a restless racehorse trainer, so we had no idea how long he'd be in there for. I stopped for food and contemplated whether to cancel a meeting I had with the journalist Brough Scott regarding a book I was writing (for a reason that escaped me at that moment) at four o'clock that afternoon.

I eventually arrived back in the yard by half-past one when Nicky phoned to say that they were on their way back. Mick had been promised that if he could eat a sandwich and keep it down, they'd let him out. He'd done so and made it into work for evening stables.

It was a cheese sandwich.

'Thanks, Nick, I'm sorry to cause you all this stress,' I said, as she made her way to her car.

'That's OK!' she said laughing. 'It felt *just* like old times!'

THE FATHERS' RACE

ATHERLEY SCHOOL SPORTS DAY, 1982

A lot happened in the spring of 1982.

I remember sitting in Auntie Sue's house somewhere near Portsmouth as the Falklands conflict kicked off. Auntie Sue was worried about Uncle Norman, and I was sitting there in my Patrick-branded Saints tracksuit drinking a Tizer I'd made in the soda stream as mum listened to her sister's concerns about the current matter in the south Atlantic. I was very proud of my Uncle Norman. He was the captain of HMS *Dumbarton Castle* no less. I even had a jumper that he'd given me with its insignia. I wore it on one of those studio-staged group family photo sessions. How exciting that he was currently driving his boat towards what Mum and Sue hoped wouldn't be a full-on war – while I hoped that it would be. My Uncle Norman, *War Hero*.

I was seven and a half. The first half of 1982 was quite a good one in my memory. I managed to contract viral meningitis and, consequently, I got to miss plenty of school and watched the entire group stages of the World Cup in Spain in splendid isolation. Things are obviously sketchy, but I had my own room in Southampton General Hospital and remember Scotland being battered by a brilliant Brazil team, and a spectacular upset involving Honduras drawing with the host nation.

I know that meningitis is a very serious condition, and I remember Mum having to call the ambulance as I was vomiting and banging my head against the toilet in anguish, apparently in panic because I'd lost my sight. I'd hate you to think I'm over-dramatising this issue, but it did actually happen, although Mum suffered far more at the time than I think I ever did. It was obviously quite serious, but kids are optimists and always retain the best parts of their childhood memories. Zico was brilliant for Brazil. Dad even took time to spend plenty of days with me in the isolation ward – although, with hindsight, he had plenty of time on his hands that summer.

My abiding memory of 1982 – Tottenham 1–0 QPR; Hoddle (pen) in a replay – occurred just before my stay in the General. It took place at my sister's school sports day. It still makes me smile and, as with Dad's attentive bedside vigil in the ensuing weeks by my hospital bed, he turned up, like a proper dad, and played a genuine part in providing us with a genuine and shared childhood memory.

This event occurred at the Atherley School. The Dell was situated about half a mile further down Hill Lane from the Atherley, and Mick turned up in his Southampton tracksuit, his Patrick trainers resplendent in the bright sunlight, and he was happy to sign autographs and mingle with everyone on what is always a memorable occasion for young children and parents alike.

Personally, I'll always remember my own school's sports days for a fat kid getting stuck in the ladder during the obstacle race, but this sports day was different. The one at my sister's school will always be remembered for the race that brought so much pride to both Nicky and me.

I'm now forty years of age. I don't have any kids, but if I ever do I know I'll never win the fathers' race. Let's look at the numbers:

I need to meet someone, have them tolerate me, put up with my eternal ramblings and ruminations on things that really don't matter, then, if they can put up with *that*, they need me to stay in touch for long enough to then tolerate my presence on a major day in our child's development. That's about ten years of acceptance. A very big ask.

Taking into account, at the very least, two years of courting, I'll be 52 years of age if my kid is going to watch me on the start line of any fathers' race. I've left things a bit too late: my child could well have a memory of me suffering a heart attack and expiring on the school running track seared into his or her brain – whereas for Nicky and I that fathers' race at the Atherley School in Southampton on that hot early summer day of 1982 was not only memorable, it was also a fucking walkover.

Nicky and I watched it head on. Our dad, fit, lean and wearing a Saints tracksuit, travelled sweetly throughout at a hack canter as a load of sweaty fat solicitors and accountants in suits toiled behind him in a plume of dust. He was a supreme athlete. He was like Frankel. Nicky won a chocolate cake. I helped her eat it that night. That was about it for 1982, though.

We were living in a flat in Bassett, a suburb north of Southampton city centre, while we were waiting for a new house on our stud farm to be finished. Mum and Dad's marriage was faltering, and I realise now that things were unravelling rather quickly. But at the time such matters were of no consequence to me, because not long after the fathers' race we learnt that our dad wouldn't be wearing a Southampton tracksuit ever again. He was released on a free transfer at the end of the season.

Sure, the impending separation of anyone's parents leaves a scar, but not being wanted by our football team – that made me feel far more upset. As much as I'd initially grown up as a

Manchester City fan, and began my sporting obsession by idol-
ising Joe Corrigan, Southampton was where we were from. It's
where we belonged. It was Reg and Avril's team, Grandma and
Grandad Channon watched Saints and always had. And now
Saints didn't want my dad. I remember asking him why.

'Lawrie says he doesn't want me any more, mate. There's
nothing we can do about that.'

He always talked to me like I was a grown-up. I remember
being very upset and wanting someone other than just me to
think that not playing for Saints was the worst thing that could
happen in the whole world. I suppose they had bigger issues
to consider, though. From then on, through the years that he
played for Norwich and a short while beyond, Dad also had a
reason to remain with us. We still had the horses, for example,
so when we moved to the stud he was in the spare room. Things
were a bit weird.

He lingered and things got quite unpleasant at times. As a
reaction, I even started to resent Southampton's manager Lawrie
McMenemy, like he was in some way responsible for my misery.
I also resented Saints for a long time. Bally stayed on as a player,
and I couldn't work that one out either. How *could* he? He was
our best friend!

I was only a kid. When Dad got a free transfer we no longer
had the season ticket above the dugout on the front row of the
upper West Stand at the Dell. That's where I used to sit on
Grandma Avril's knee every other Saturday when things were
great with the world. I watched the *QE2* and the *Canberra* return
from the Falklands at Southampton Docks that summer with
Avril, though, and Uncle Norman came home safe and sound.
Now *that* is something to be grateful for – I know that today. I
also know it's far more important than your parents' impend-

ing divorce, or the fact that you can no longer watch your dad playing football on Grandma Avril's knee.

I'm a middle-aged man today, but at seven and a half years of age, Dad winning the fathers' race and that chocolate cake I shared with Nicky seemed to be all that really mattered. A special memory. Our dad, fit and lean; a picture of health.

THE CRASH, PART 2

NOTTINGHAM UNIVERSITY HOSPITAL, AUGUST – SEPTEMBER 2008

Just a few short hours after seeing the police walking across the driveway and being told of the car crash, I was being shown through to the Intensive Care Unit at Nottingham University Hospital. It would have been in the early hours of the morning by then. I had no idea what I'd be faced with. Jill decided it would be best if we split up: she'd visit Jack first in the children's ward, so I went in to see my dad.

He was barely recognisable. His head looked to be twice its usual size, his jaw on the left side was folded up on itself, over-lapping. The swelling was so severe that his ears stuck *into* his head. Shocking stuff. He was sedated but knew I was there. We only said a few words.

'You all right?' I held his hand.

He nodded. 'Where's Jack? How's Jack?' He was a mess and all over the shop – a mixture of pain, shock and worry. A husky, cracked voice.

'Jack's OK. He bounced, he's not an old git like you. Jill's with him now, she'll be here in a bit.'

'He'll be OK, though, won't he?'

'He'll be fine. Honestly, Dad, he's in much better shape than you.' I was telling the truth in that regard. Jack was *definitely* better than the old man, and I'd not seen him yet – only 15 years old and I can't imagine what he'd been through that afternoon. A damaged knee and a few cracked vertebrae was all I knew at that stage, along with the concussion that accompanied such a serious impact. All I cared about was that he wasn't critical, unlike the bloke before me. He then said something so sad, but so typically up front that I lost it for a bit. 'Tim's gone.' He closed his eyes. Gutted. I hadn't known if he knew or not, but he clearly did. They wouldn't confirm it to me, but Mick knew. He was there.

It took a while for me to say anything after that. I just wanted to know one thing. 'Dad, *listen to me*. I knew I'd be all right when I got smashed up. How do *you* feel? I always knew I'd be OK even though everyone else was worried. I need you to tell me how bad *you* feel you are.'

'I'll be OK.'

That was all he could manage, but I believed him. I believed him because I'd always believed *in* him, and he knew what I meant. He'd live.

The loss of Tim would take some time to get over. I don't think any of us know what that feels like unless we experience it for ourselves. I didn't even know how it had happened at that stage.

Jill and I changed shifts, as we would do for the days and weeks to come, and I was soon standing over Jack in the children's ward. What a ridiculous sight he was. He might have qualified as a child at 15, but by then he was a big lad, almost six feet, hairy legs hanging out of the bed. There were glow-stars on the ceiling above him, and paintings of Andy Pandy and Rupert the Bear on the wall.

'Tim's dead,' was all he said. I didn't know what to say to him. He was smashed up and also heavily sedated, but I really couldn't do or say anything to help. Only 15 and he'd been conscious throughout the whole thing. I've never asked him to tell me about it, even now. I could probably have been a better brother.

I slept just down the hall that night, and the police were in attendance the next morning early enough. I remember them arriving because I was on the phone to trainer Jeremy Noseda's office at the time. I was supposed to be filming some Highclere syndicate horses with him that morning but decided I'd better cancel. I never did finish that contract.

The police knew very little apart from the facts before them: Tim had been driving with Mick in the passenger seat and Jack in the back when they veered off the M1 just past junction 24 and collided with a concrete bridge, the pillar of the overpass. No other vehicle was involved. It would take some time but it eventually transpired that Tim had suffered heart failure at the wheel. There was nothing anyone could have done to predict that.

For the next few days I just hung around, waiting and hoping for an upturn in both Mick and Jack's conditions. The owner and renowned gambler Harry Findlay, who had been at the sales with them that week, paid a visit and brought a load of magazines for Jack to read – *FHM*, *Loaded*, all the lads' magazines with their front covers featuring scantily clad models. Like Jack, they had little place in that children's ward. That raised a laugh, though. Harry is a good man, but then again everyone was so kind, and the phone rang constantly.

Over the next 48 hours Mick went into surgery to have his jaw wired and his right arm pinned. His breathing was a real struggle due to his broken ribs, and he looked abysmal. It took several days for him to come to terms with what had happened. The good news was that Jack, despite a horrific knee injury and several cracked vertebrae, was making giant strides. Kids, eh?

I felt very lucky that Mick and Jack were still with us. I felt guilty for that because of what Tim's family were left with. A big hole that couldn't be filled.

When I went into the ICU on the Monday morning to see the old man he was still sedated, still in and out of consciousness, but he'd improved over the last four days. He was speaking a little more but remained incredibly sad and understandably disorientated. He then said something that I'll never forget: 'What day is it today?'

'Monday,' I said.

'Phone Joe.'

'Joe?'

'Yeah. Phone Joe.'

'Joe's got everything in hand, Dad. Don't worry about the horses.'

'It's work day tomorrow. Phone Joe and tell him that he needs to work Youmzain round the seven. Make sure Sam rides him and tell Candy to go a good one on Alfred in front.'

He was in intensive care and still trying to train horses. I can't think of many people who would be able to focus on that after the last few days. But *he* did.

Youmzain was a proper horse. A bit of a rogue and notoriously difficult to win with, but he'd given us some of the best days imaginable during that period regardless of how frustrating he could be. He was a Group 1 winner but a bit of a herd animal, able to travel with any horse at the top level but only putting himself at the head of affairs for a brief, glimpsing moment. He'd finished second in the Prix de l'Arc de Triomphe the previous season, second in the Coronation Cup at Epsom this time around, and won a Group 1 in France only two months earlier that summer. It was time for him to get ready again for the Arc, the most prestigious race for middle-distance horses in Europe. He was Mick's pride and joy. A pain in the arse perhaps, very frustrating but very talented, and we'd managed to buy him as a yearling for 33,000 guineas. For the sort of money he was winning, that represented a pittance.

I did as I was told and Joe Tuite worked Youmzain accordingly, reporting back to the boss that work morning went well the following day. He did a great job, Joe Tuite.

Whilst there were plenty of good wishes, my phone also rang with journalists wanting updates on Mick's condition. Some were well intentioned although I suspected that others weren't. As a result I made extra-sure that the staff in the ICU allowed *nobody* in unless either Jill or I said so first. I was probably a bit abrupt and more than a little paranoid, but I knew Mick would be mortified if anyone saw him in the state he was in. They knew the score.

One afternoon, though, I returned to the ICU after having lunch downstairs in the hospital canteen when a very ruffled nurse told me that Mick had a visitor that she was unable to stop from going in.

'I said that *nobody* should be allowed in unless they are family or close friends!' I snapped.

'I know, Mr Channon, but he insists he's family and was very forceful. We didn't have any other option.'

I walked round the corner to see a bearded man standing over Mick, open-neck shirt and tattoos on his forearms. He was shouting, 'I'm telling you, boy, they've got you in the right place here! Triple heart bypass they done to me and it was the best thing I could have done. It's my local hospital, you see, and I'm glad it is. They don't fuck about in here!'

I sighed with relief. 'It's OK,' I said to the nurse who had followed me, 'that's my dad's Uncle John.'

Now, I'd only met Uncle John once before, when my Grandad Jack died back in 2001, and he's a force of nature; a plain-speaking, no-nonsense former navy man. Most of his stories involve him using the phrase, 'Well, I hit him, didn't I?' at some point. He's a bit confrontational, Uncle John.

The week grandad Jack died the whole family descended on West Ilsley, primarily to gather around Grandma. Fifty-nine years they'd been married and they only spent a handful of nights apart, a proper old school marriage of devotion and contentment. I'd come down from Manchester and was in the office with Mick when one of the lads came in and said that there had been a spot of trouble on the driveway: 'A bloke was driving down with a caravan and I told him it was private property, boss.'

'So?' asked Mick.

'Well, he got out of the car, told me to fuck off and then threatened to hit me. He said he was here to visit his sister.'

'Oh, that's all right,' said Mick. 'That'll be my uncle John.'

You get the picture.

After a week or so, Mick was moved to a high dependency ward, a sure sign that he was out of danger, but the morphine was beginning to mess with his head a little. While Jack was discharged after ten days or so, Mick's recuperation would take a little longer, and I was lucky to have Nicky on hand after Jill was forced to return home having come down with the flu. Things remained stressful but Mick provided moments of high comedy as he believed he was perfectly fine by then and he ought to get back to work. On a particularly blustery day he asked Nicky why they were on a train as the trees outside were swaying in the wind. Then, when we'd put his mind at ease about where he was, we told him we were leaving for the day but would be back in the morning. I said goodbye and began to walk away when he pulled Nicky to one side: 'Nicky, come here, I want a word.'

I left them to it. I thought Mick was going to say something touching and personal. Morphine can have a strange effect on people, even someone like the old man. When she came out, between tears she told me what he'd said. It went something like this,

'What is it, Dad?'

'Get Jill outside with the car.'

'What?'

'We're getting me out of here. They're trying to keep me here but I'm fine now.'

'Dad, you're hooked up to a million machines behind you. You need them for now.'

'We'll *buy* them! Just get Jill outside with the car, we'll leave now!'

I ought to stress that Nicky's tears were of laughter, although we couldn't wait for the morphine to be taken away.

Mick didn't want to see anybody apart from close family and his closest friends. Nicky was there, along with Phil. I told Phil how I was being pestered by a Welsh bloke claiming to be from the *News of the World* who kept offering thirty grand for a photo of the old man in hospital. He'd said it was for a charity of our choice but the implication wasn't lost on me. I expected Phil to share my disgust.

'Thirty grand, eh?' He pulled out his mobile and took a picture of his battered brother with it. 'Right, I'll see you later!' and he walked off laughing. Bizarrely, we did a lot of laughing that week, the sort of necessary laughter that is common at funeral wakes but often seems misplaced. You can't spend all day every day contemplating the sadness.

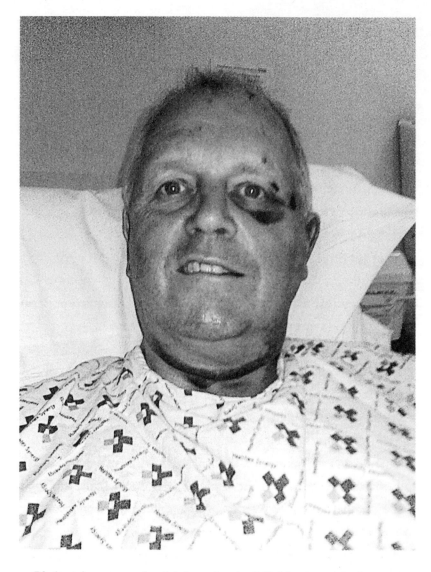

If there's one major high point in Mick's recovery it was an unannounced visit he received a week or so after leaving the Nottingham University Hospital. Just before he left he was understandably low and insisting that he needed to get home and get back to work. Throughout the whole episode he was adamant that he didn't want anyone to see him, he didn't want anyone's sympathy and he just wanted out. But he wasn't allowed to go that far; he was out of the high dependency unit, but he still needed to be under observation. As a compromise, he agreed to be transferred to a private hospital just outside of Nottingham while Nicky and I remained in a hotel in the city.

A few days after he'd arrived there, I heard laughter as I entered his room. Standing there was Asa Hartford, Mick's former team-mate at Manchester City and Norwich. Mick was smiling for the first time since the crash three weeks before. I'm so grateful that Asa ignored what I said to him on the phone. I was very grateful that my dad was going to be OK.

That was the moment. Two old friends sharing a laugh and talking about Mick's physical recovery, blatantly avoiding the emotional trauma he'd endured; the elephant in the room who was shuffling uncomfortably.

We returned home five days later. I never returned to my media job, and Piccolo Productions folded as I gradually became an assistant trainer. I wasn't appointed; I just blended into the business at West Ilsley Stables.

Youmzain finished second in that year's Arc, as he would the year after that. A remarkable horse who won over three million quid before he retired to stud. Mick has many critics, but that was a great training performance by a man who never took his eye off the ball, even when he was in intensive care.

But, of course, there was Tim's funeral to deal with, which I attended on Mick's behalf. It took place at Raunds, Northamptonshire, 'up the crem' as Tim often referred to it when he would discuss his demise in the offhand and jovial manner that he was renowned for.

I still think of Tim, with his weathered face and his ill-fitting trousers, smoking a fag and dreaming of the next Innit, Checkit, Katchit or Missit. That was Tim's trademark for naming horses.

Back home a month later

If he ever had a dud he'd often lament, 'I don't think it's very good, mine. Should have been called "Fuckit".'

He was a rascal was Tim. He always had a plan and was always scheming away. He was only 63 but had crammed plenty in. Looking back at the madness of that whole saga it feels quite surreal to have been there. One minute we were on the gallops discussing the forthcoming sales and two days later you're faced with police walking up the drive.

Tim was gone; no more lunches in the Crown & Horns after work mornings, enjoying a pint and listening to him getting more and more excited as he convinced himself that his latest cheap yearling purchase was about to beat the world. A couple more pints and he'd be talking about how much he'd be prepared to sell it for. Tim Corby; a dreamer and a schemer. A fine and funny man.

A LOW EBB

THURSDAY 9 JULY 2015

We've not been pulling up any trees with the horses, just chipping in with winners here and there at gaff tracks but I've been aware for some time that I need to get some perspective on life and get away from the endless pressure attached to such a silly existence.

It's two days after the vomiting jamboree that led to the John Radcliffe Hospital, and today I found myself heading to Newmarket's July Course, where Bossy Guest faced what, on paper, seemed to be a straightforward task in a Listed race over a mile. You may recall that he finished strongly after a luckless run at Royal Ascot in a Group 3 over seven furlongs, so a drop into lesser company over a mile seemed like a logical step. Consequently, he went off at odds-on. That's all well and good when things are going well but pessimism abounds between my ears at present, and I drove up there on my own full of anxiety with a crippling lack of both professional and personal confidence nagging in my head. I was dreading it. Mick, understandably after the trauma of the previous 48 hours, didn't feel up to it so I headed there alone, shot to bits and full of doubt.

I'm never like this. I love a pint and a laugh, and people on the whole (I hope) are pleased to see me. For once, though, I didn't want to see anyone else. That's quite hard at Newmarket's July meeting, one of the mid-summer's major sporting and social occasions. Everyone seemed to have a drink in their hand and a smile on their face, while I was barely able to make eye contact with anyone. What worsened my nerves was the world and his wife coming up to me telling me Bossy Guest was a certainty. I'm more than well aware that there is no such thing these days and the season so far, coupled with my worry over the old man's health and a withering lack of sleep, had made me irritable, ratty and a right grumpy bastard. I just wanted to saddle the horse, win the race and bugger off.

I'm not usually a bad ally in adversity. I'd prepared myself to step up after the trip to hospital to make sure that things functioned as efficiently as they always do, and that morning I was in earlier than usual. I went into the office at about half-five and found the old man sitting at his desk, making entries in the calendar.

'Mornin', boy!'

'What are you doing here?'

'Ah, couldn't sleep so I thought I'd get on with things.'

This gave me the hump. I was knackered just watching him throwing up the previous evening and here he was, not looking too bad if I'm honest, but surely in no fit state to oversee the horses. But he did and we got on with things. As we always do. Perhaps he *does* think he's immortal.

Predictably enough, Bossy Guest was away slowly, as is his wont, but instead of there being a fast pace in the race, they crawled, and rather than going past tiring horses at the finish they quickened away up the front. Bossy was never going to win and managed only third – one of those horrible experiences that leaves you watching on helplessly in a bubble of trepidation. At halfway I knew we had no chance, and even Ryan Moore said as much as he dismounted. I tried to act interested in what he was saying but I was just hollowed out. I left as soon as I could.

How ridiculous. It's horseracing, it's not important in the real world.

It's probably because I don't come from a racing background that my paranoia is so heightened. Paying thirty grand for a horse that turns out to be useless rots my mind, for example. I feel sympathy for owners who see that sort of money evaporate inside six months, while they still have bills to pay to keep this animal in the manner to which it has become accustomed. It's ludicrous, silly and absurd in so many ways. But we're all big boys, and I'm old enough and intelligent enough to know that such pitfalls are the norm rather than the exception in racing, so I really ought to grow a pair and stop feeling so dismal, although I know it creeps up on everyone from time to time. I remember one morning late last year on the gallops when Mick turned to me after reading something less than complimentary in the paper.

'It doesn't matter what I do at times,' he said. 'To *them*, I'll always be a footballer. A fucking outsider.'

The demoralising nature of training racehorses affects even the hardiest of souls, I suppose.

JAADU

GLORIOUS GOODWOOD, THURSDAY 30 JULY 2015

July has been particularly dismal. I've been racing almost every day and gone along with a heavy heart. There were a few days spent pulling ragwort in the paddocks with the rest of the lads at West Ilsley and, although it's bloody hard work, it felt like a holiday compared to the days of disappointment at the track. Mick mucked in as much as he could but he soon got back in the wagon to offer words of encouragement: 'You've got to pull the fuckers out by the roots, otherwise they'll just come back again! No fucker bothers dealing with this stuff except us, only we seem to care about livestock. It's all along the roads and nobody does fuck all about it! Lazy bastards!' His moaning echoed across the fields as we chortled to ourselves. It seemed never-ending; a constant tirade against the world.

Something happened today that should have improved morale among the ragwort-pullers, though. For today was a good day.

Remember Jaadu, the two-year-old who worked brilliantly at the start of the season, back when optimism abounded and all seemed well with the world? Remember when Adie, the Mancunian foster parent made his unexpected but much welcome appearance at West Ilsley? Yeah? Good, because things came right for us today.

'You've got to pull the fuckers out by the roots!'

If I'm honest, Jaadu's been one of the main reasons that I've started to doubt myself for the lion's share of this season. He's very good, but the start to his career has caused only blame, bollockings and bemusement (no change there, then). I don't claim to be a genius, but I'm certainly not stupid, and his first three runs saw him finish unplaced, almost an also ran. It was this young horse that had left me totally bereft of confidence – in both my own judgement and the quality of our two-year-olds on whom we're so dependent if we're to unearth a good one.

Jaadu romps to victory

Well, today Jaadu romped home at Glorious Goodwood. I backed him as well. I had £100 each way on him, a huge bet for me, but I've recently started thinking that I either back my own judgement or curl up and go under. I'm being dramatic there, because in the working environment in which I exist giving up just isn't an option. All I'd be left with is the prospect of getting even more depressed than I was at Newmarket. That would not only be unbearable, it would also make for a dismal, depressing and dreadful book, so thank fuck I was right about Jaadu.

The thing is, his first three runs earmarked him as being mentally retarded when it came to the demands of racing. In spite of the raw ability he shows at home he simply couldn't do himself justice. And as a result of running so poorly, he'd been given a handicap mark of 71.

If you're capable of making a distinction as to what this means in the baffling world of horseracing, 71 is a moderate weight allocation befitting of a moderate horse. A top two-year-old would be rated, say, 110, and Jaadu, to my mind, is at the very least a 90 horse, and today was his first run in a nursery handicap for juveniles. Therefore, he was carrying almost 20 pounds less than he should do on the ability I'd seen at home. Which meant that he should piss up.

And he did.

I'm not a great gambler and usually bet on course in cash, so placing £200 on a horse is a big deal to me. I dispatched my mate Ged, who was spending the week with me, to the rails to place the bet and wandered over to the unsaddling enclosure to watch the race on a big screen that is always in place during Goodwood's showpiece occasion.

Clever people take an early price on the morning of a race, before the market shortens on a fancied horse, but I'm not a clever man, and betting plays an insignificant role in my life. Today was about me being right. The season up to this point has been a shambles and if this horse didn't win, personal confidence in my entire existence, the sleepless nights of fretting and worry would be confirmed. How melodramatic does that sound?

Very.

That is both true and pathetic.

We've worked so hard for so little reward for months now. Mick's work ethic is exceptional, but he's taken on the mentality of a man trying to flatten a sheet of corrugated iron with a hammer – like Father Ted trying to fix the dent in his car. He's a relentless workaholic who insists that hard work will always reap rewards, but it's been even harder work to work alongside him of late.

He's right, though: results do come.

When Jaadu streaked clear of the field, not once did I shout and not once did I become animated. The horse had to win and

I just hoped it was a sign that the weeks of endless misery were coming to a close. He won at 12/1, although Ged had managed to get 14/1 and I would be picking up two grand. OK, so I missed the 25/1 that a more astute gambler would have enjoyed earlier on in the day, but it was my personal confidence that soared way ahead of my bank balance this afternoon. That feels incredibly important right now.

MALABAR

GLORIOUS GOODWOOD, FRIDAY 31 JULY 2015

Jaadu's romp yesterday seems to have started the ball rolling, and today Malabar, the only filly in a race otherwise full of colts, romped home in the Group 3 Bonhams Thoroughbred Stakes. A thrilling feeling, just reward for a talented filly, and all credit to the old man. He fitted her in a visor for the first time and she looked completely transformed. She's not very big and Mick was convinced that she was being intimidated in her races. The headgear gave her confidence and Silvestre de Sousa gave her the perfect ride. The feeling of relief was overwhelming.

I think today might well signal the turning of the tide. As I said, Jaadu's win certainly gave me confidence that I wasn't completely clueless, and today Malabar murdered a strong-looking field, coming home nearly three lengths clear of the next best. That was a magic moment. We were standing on the grass on the corner of the grandstand and screamed her home in the usual dignity-stripping fashion, a routine rounded off by Mick jumping all over Malabar's owner Julia Aisbitt and then the pair of us sharing a very brief and typically awkward hug together.

A win live on Channel 4 means that everyone thought we were marvellous again. Being on the telly reminds everyone you're still around, and I was very proud of the old man. Sure, we'd

Malabar comes in

been at loggerheads on Wednesday because I thought Bossy
Guest should have run in the same race, but Mick chose to keep
them apart, so Bossy ran against older horses in the Group 1
Sussex Stakes instead. That led to not only a fraught start to the
week but another sacking for Charlie Bishop, but that's a distant
memory now.

The win also goes some way to making a mockery of the joker
who covered over the sign to the stables with his own homemade
one. It might have been a member of staff, or possibly a disgrun-
tled punter, but it must have taken some time and effort. Sten-
cilled onto a sheet of painted plywood the exact dimensions of
the existing sign, it read: 'West Ilsley Donkey Sanctuary'. It hung
there looking like a parody of the opening titles of *Fawlty Towers*.

Cheeky bastard.

That too seems all in the past, and I feel as though the misery
is now a side salad as opposed to the main course. A good drink

A lot of time and effort went into making that sign

is always needed, of course, and we had more than one when apprehended by trainer George Baker in the car park afterwards. A great day and I didn't have a penny on her. My bet on Jaadu yesterday would see me well for a while and, besides, as I've already said, I'm not much of a gambler.

There was this one time, though . . .

THE BET

THURSDAY 11 SEPTEMBER 2014

It's only a short time ago, but this was a day when time stood still.

On a fairly innocuous Thursday morning I was reading the *Racing Post*, looking through our runners and trying to get a grip on them all. We had plenty scattered around the country at Chepstow, Doncaster, Epsom and Wolverhampton. It then occurred to me that at least six would be placed. I was so certain of it that I told all of my mates that I thought they ought to have a bit of fun with them.

I sent the same information to my friend Marc Middlemiss in the north-east. He has a share in a couple of horses and often tips me over the edge when we enjoy a day's racing and a night out. York is one of our favourite haunts. It's far enough away to justify stopping over and we often share a hotel room together, like a modern-day version of Morecambe and Wise. The trouble with this arrangement, though, is that Middler is ten years younger than me. A night out with him can be both hilarious yet debilitating. I often have to sneak out unseen and retreat to the hotel when my stamina runs out. I can't drink like I used to.

As irreverent gamblers, the pair of us had always enjoyed a string of near misses that allowed us to wax lyrical in the pub about 'our day'. Our dreamy conversations I'm sure are familiar to many: 'We'll have our day, son, it's only a matter of time, I can feel it – it's just around the corner.' That eternal pub promise that never comes true.

'Our day' continued to be 'just around the corner', especially for Middler, who is one of life's great optimists. He's one of those lads who just makes things happen – a smart guy who works hard but can't help going a bit mental from time to time. It might be the Geordie gene in him. I went out with a Newcastle girl for quite some time (by my standards), and she was quite mad but incredibly smart. Middler is the same.

This was the text I sent to him:

Each way chances:
Epsom: Harlequin Striker; Gratzie
Donny: Persun; Shore Step
Chepstow: Jontleman
Wolves: Al Manaal
Don't thank me, just send me a bottle of Krug.

This was what came back (it helps if you read it with a Geordie accent):

Bloody hell, ha, ha. Right, I'll see what kind of bankrupting accumulator
I can get on these bad boys this afternoon. Nice to see you're into your
fine bubbly these days, my personal preference to celebrate a life-changing
betting coup is Blue Nun – the magnum edition.

It was the usual nonsense optimism that raised a smile with the following confirmation coming through half an hour later. Adopt Geordie accent again:

Right, mate, I've chucked £174 at them for us. Basically, if they all win we'll have exceeded the maximum payout and will be sharing a million quid. But if we'd been more astute in heinghnsight [sic] we probably could of saved £3 by down-staking so the payout came out at exactly a mill. But we're not playing games here, son! COME ON YA FUCKERS!!!

I thought £87 each was a bit steep for such an optimistic bet, but Middler knows more about betting than I do. He's got an account on the internet and everything – far smarter than me.

I left for Epsom and thought little more of it, especially when our first selection, Persun, was beaten in the nursery handicap at Doncaster. When the first leg of a six-timer goes down, a reassuring sense of the usual shattered dream arrives with its all too familiar grace. The fact that Harlequin Striker (9/2) and Gratzie (7/1) won the first two at Epsom made me feel a bit daft – why didn't we do a clever combination bet? In racing terms, we'd had a good day up to that point. Our only two on the card at Epsom had won and I was asked to do an interview on television for Racing UK.

I've mastered the art of saying plenty without any real gravitas, depth or form analysis when I'm interviewed on the telly. It just seems so absurd that people would be interested in my views. I've developed the art of hiding deep-rooted paranoia behind what I imagine to be a cheeky grin and a 'what would I know about it anyway?' manner of delivery. It works for me and I'm happy with it as long as I never see it or get any feedback from anybody. My Granada days are always at the back of my mind.

I left the parade ring having lost track of time only to see the last furlong of the seven-furlong handicap at Chepstow. Jontleman won by a head at odds of 14/1. I reached for my phone. 'Where do we stand, Middler?'

He came back with a glimmer of hope: 'I'm not sure, mate, but we've done a Heinz variety bet which means we've got every possible combination covered and it's getting a little bit interesting. Let's just see how Shore Step gets on at Donny and I'll try to get my head round it. I've been in meetings all afternoon.'

I came home on the horsebox that afternoon and we were battling through Bracknell traffic when we listened to the commentary of Shore Step in the 5.35 at Doncaster on the phone. It was an eighteen-runner handicap over six furlongs. It was obviously a tight contest, with a million horses being mentioned in a frantic finale, but '. . . and Shore Step gets back up on the line!' was all I needed to hear. He'd won at odds of 11/1. I was just numb. There was no celebration, just a shaky hand fumbling for Middler's number.

'Middler, *what the fuck is going on?*'

'I diven't nah, mate! We've fucking nailed it is all I know. We've got to be at least two grand up! We'll be taking that out of the pot anyway, but if Al Manaal wins at Wolves we'll make a killing!' Middler was excited.

So was I now I think about it. 'Can't you be a bit more accurate than that? What could we be looking at?'

'Well, if I'm right and she wins we'll be on about twenty grand!'

'Fuck off!' I said.

'Honestly! I fucking told ya we'd have our day, son – this could be it!'

The horsebox got back to the yard at six o'clock. Al Manaal was running in the 6.15 at Wolverhampton over seven furlongs. She was a 10/1 shot. The old man and finance director Gill Hedley were in the office grinning madly, and by this stage I was a bit of a wreck: 'Twenty grand! Middler reckons we're on for twenty grand if Al Manaal wins this.'

'I reckon it'll be more than twenty grand,' was all Mick said.

I couldn't face watching it with them so I went home and opened the only bottle of beer I had in the fridge.

A horse called Aragosta was the warm 6/4 favourite and Al Manaal received only a fleeting mention in the preliminaries. I'm not a cosmic person but I certainly had a strange sense of inner calm that told me something ludicrous was about to happen. (When I was lying in Bristol Royal Infirmary I had a similar sense of certainty that things were in my favour.) 'This'll win,' I thought. Not because of form, not because of the track or the draw in stall two being in our favour. I just sort of expected it.

They jumped off and Al Manaal, with Charlie Bishop in the saddle, was always in touch with the leaders while Aragosta was out the back. All I could see was the two horses in the eight-runner field. Off the final bend, Al Manaal kicked for home with the main danger at least seven lengths behind. Our horse hit the front a furlong from home and then the favourite began clawing back the deficit. Time stood still, my mind raced and all I could think was, 'Just my fucking luck, this will get chinned on the line.' I began to lean to my right, willing the line to come as Aragosta kept coming and Al Manaal began to paddle, exhausted from her efforts, blissfully unaware of the importance of her final desperate strides in a Class 4 handicap on the all-weather track at Wolverhampton.

A photo-finish.

She won by a nose.

I went mental.

How much had we won? Had this really happened? After all, this was just another of me and Middler's pipedream silly forecast bets. They *never* come off.

I ran to the office screaming like a lunatic. I could barely dial Middler's number. Once I did, he picked it up immediately. The

Celebrating the bet at York's Ebor meeting. Things got messy

computer had quickly calculated our winnings and he just said to me, matter of factly, 'Are you sitting down?'

My mind boggled, I couldn't believe it. An ordinary Thursday had turned into a day that would make life a hell of a lot easier. There was only one thing for it: everyone down the Harrow and the drinks were on me. I got on my bike and headed down there (this was not going to be a night for driving). I was numb, happy and completely scrambled. There was one thing I had to do. She picked up the phone as I was cycling past the village hall: 'Mum! Where do you want to go?' I was jabbering like a lunatic.

'What?'

'Take whoever you want, go wherever you want, and I don't care what it costs.'

She was confused at first but I managed to gabble my way through the details. Our five horses had won at odds of over 54,000/1. A payout of £81,272 between Middler and me for an outlay of £174.

And my mum went to Mauritius.

BRISTOL ROYAL INFIRMARY

SUNDAY 14 MAY 1995

MICK CHANNON KID BUSTS HIS NECK SLEEPWALKING

Soccer star's lad falls 20ft off roof

Plunge . . . Michael Channon

The *Sun*, May 1995. Typical inaccuracy – it was 40ft

'There's a phone call for you, Michael.'

'I don't care.'

'You'll want to take this one, so don't be so grumpy. We'll wheel you over to reception.'

'I don't fucking care.'

'You're taking this phone call.'

The previous nine days had been a bit of a blur if I'm honest. That's morphine for you.

I'd been admitted to Bristol's Royal Infirmary in the early hours of 5 May after falling off that roof on Redland Road. I'd had a brilliant time at the University of the West of England

(UWE) up until that point. I was as fit as was humanly possible after my trial at Southampton, the sort of lean and youthful fitness that nobody appreciates at that time of their lives. I was also very cocky, arrogant and consummately sure of myself. I was 20 years old, and I'm not a fan of the obnoxious lad I was back then, so full of opinions about things I knew nothing about, living off a student grant that technically I was entitled to having enrolled at university as a single-parent child – a situation both as laughable and preposterous as my behaviour and conduct.

I embraced university life completely. I was a brilliant student: I played football, met countless friends and did zero studying. After being shown the door by Bally at Southampton, I thought that university would give me time to work out what I actually wanted to do. It had turned out that football wasn't my forte after all, so I just decided to get into a university that was in a big city. And Bristol was a great place for students.

There was plenty of football, always played on a Wednesday, and always a good social scene on a Wednesday evening. In fact, once I'd bumped into two lads from Wolverhampton, Andy Porter and Richard Buchan, I didn't even stay at my initial student digs in Fishponds for the final month of my tenancy agreement prior to Christmas. I slept on their floor in the far trendier area of Clifton – and there were plenty of pubs in Clifton and down 'Blackboy Hill', or Whiteladies Road, as it's officially known.

My stay at Bristol's Royal Infirmary only came about because I'd gone a bit bonkers, if I'm honest. I can see that now.

By describing myself as a 'brilliant student' I'm referring to the culture I embraced because I certainly never studied. *Never.* My girlfriend Anna was at Cardiff University, so that was handy. I'd met and fallen head over heels for her at Peter Symonds College in Winchester during my A levels but, while she was not only gorgeous, kind, conscientious and intent on getting a degree, I'd ignored that side of things and got properly stuck in. In my defence, which is flimsy, I'll agree, my choice of academic study hardly helped. I was basically in a position where my B-, C- and D-graded A levels meant that I had to take up whatever spaces were available after the successful and ambitious A level academics had already accepted theirs. Therefore, I took whatever I could – as long as it didn't sound like hard work. Don't judge me, I was only 20.

I opted for a degree in social and media studies, whatever that was. I guess I was attracted by the media angle of it, but the course turned out to be a mismatch of several facets of study that I had zero interest in – aka total bollocks. At one point I spent three days in a youth hostel on the Brecon Beacons analysing moss samples. How that came under the umbrella of social or media studies I cannot fathom. Perhaps I got on the wrong minibus.

There were times when media was studied, but even that was a demoralising experience of analytical nonsense. The course was based in the UWE's campus in Fishponds, about six miles from the proper university, which explains why my digs were so far from the raucous nightlife of the city centre. After our lectures were delivered in the mornings the students were expected to partake in discursive seminars about the presentations they'd just received. These were weird affairs that I'd treat with disdain and cynicism, basically because I was totally at odds with my fellow students. I'd hate to think I'm reverting to stereotyping individuals but the social and media studies course at the University of the West of England in 1995 seemed to be dominated by angry, middle-aged divorced women with severe depression who hated men. Those seminars weren't much fun.

There was one that sticks in my mind. We were discussing the banal, feel-good yet extravagant genres of film and television in the 1980s when *The A-Team* was mentioned as a typical example of the time. For some reason, I became excitedly animated and offered more input than I had done since enrolling on the course the previous September. I spewed forth all of my enthusiasm and appreciation of how excited I'd be on a Friday evening; about how I'd rush home for my tea ahead of the latest episode featuring Howling Mad Murdock's newest alter ego and B. A. Baracus's unbridled thuggery, backed up by the Faceman's latest con trick providing the A-Team with sufficient intelligence with which they could right the wrongs initiated by a team of con artists, bullies or downright rotters that week. I *loved The A-Team*.

For half an hour I then had to listen about how a male-dominated society in the 1980s polluted artistic culture and how masculine insecurity during this period was symbolised by George Peppard's character Hannibal Smith constantly smoking a cigar. It took a while for the penny to drop, if I'm honest, because in my mind I was still reliving the montages of how a blowtorch and a bit of corrugated iron could convert a tractor into a tank. I'll never forget the sentence that jolted me back to my senses:

'It's quite clearly a penis,' a woman said.

'What is?' I asked.

'The cigar is a clear embodiment of male insecurity. It symbolises the ethos of the time.' There was widespread agreement with loads of nodding and murmurs of agreement. I was in a massive minority. No wonder I always had the chair right in the corner.

'Are you saying that George Peppard spent the whole of my childhood giving blow jobs to a cigar?'

'Yes, that's what his character represented. And he still does.'

That was the last seminar or lecture I ever attended at UWE.

It was only March.

Not to worry, though, the UWE had got through to the quarter-finals of the BUSA Cup and there was plenty to look forward to. I was the best player at university, and although we got knocked out in the quarter-finals against Sheffield University after a replay, I'd met loads of good lads, and we'd usually all end up in Kickers nightclub on Whiteladies Road before a curry then staggering back home before doing it all again, as and when finances would allow.

I was best mates with Neil Pugh by then, a lad from Chester and a big Manchester City fan. He was old, about 25 I think, but he too, like me, loved Joe Corrigan. He lived with his sister, who was based in Bristol just up the road from the third-floor flat I'd moved into on Redland Road. Our local was the Jersey Lily, and I was just down the road from Richard and Andy. That meant I was right where I wanted to be: near the nightlife and my friends and a long way away from my university campus. We played a lot of Donkey Kong on the Nintendo.

My flat at 144D Redland Road was a massive period building, only a five-minute walk from the Jersey Lily. The flat itself was tiny, and I shared it with some old bloke whose name I can't recall. He was an art student, probably about 26 or 27 years of age. My room had a mattress on the floor and a telly–video combo that sat on a cardboard box at the end of the bed. There was a table and chair in the corner, with *Loaded* and *FourFourTwo* magazines on them. The kitchen was particularly tiny. I grilled a lot of fish fingers in that kitchen, and washing up in that top-floor attic flat offered incredible views across Bristol, perched as it was, high up above the city. The kitchen window jutted out as an extension through the roof, and there was a skylight above it with a pivoting window allowing access to the roof courtesy of a small ladder. My landlord was a vicar who allowed me to pay my deposit off along with the rent. I loved living in that flat.

There was never much need for an excuse to go out, but 4 May 1995 was the twenty-first birthday of a lad who lived in the flat beneath me. Everyone in that building was invited, and although I wasn't exactly friends with them it was a Thursday night and there wasn't much else on. They were nice people and the girls on the ground floor were a bit of a mystery to me, although Pughie knew one of them quite well. We all went out that evening: a few pints in the pub, then on to an Italian restaurant where I had spaghetti bolognaise and we started drinking red wine. We got pissed. I got very pissed.

I'd spent the previous day on the rooftop enjoying the unusual heatwave of that spring, and I managed to get sunburnt all down my right-hand side in the process, so when I got home from the Italian restaurant the skylight and the sun lounger on the roof seemed like the logical place to sleep. Sure, there were no balustrades, but it was stiflingly hot. 'It'll be fine,' I thought. I do remember there being a bottle of vodka. I thought little of my sleepwalking habits, which had begun as a small boy but had become more commonplace as a drinking adolescent.

You know what happened next.

After the adrenaline, the panic, the ambulance, the Accident & Emergency and the briefly sober moment of giving the staff all of my contact details, the next thing I remember is blacking out.

Then I remember looking at a fluorescent strip light.

For ages.

My head was taped to a board when a nurse eventually leant over me and explained that we'd be going down for some X-rays to find out if any more damage had been done 'as a precaution'.

I was very thirsty. I remember being wheeled down, and then I identified understated but clearly well-placed panic as I over-heard voices saying that a specialist was needed. I remember being left somewhere else and looking at yet another fluorescent strip light.

For ages.

It soon became apparent to me that I was in a very serious condition. I'd managed to break six ribs on my right side that had punctured the lung, which was bleeding alarmingly. A frac-tured hip, a broken elbow, a broken jaw and numerous lacera-tions – including my left ear, which was cut in half – didn't help matters either. I was basically in tatters, and the precautionary X-rays revealed I had also broken my neck – none of this made things easy for the staff at the BRI. I was really thirsty, though, but apart from that I didn't notice the hangover, which should have been horrendous.

From there the days became hazed, minutes became hours and visits became infrequently frequent. I can't accurately recall the chronological order of events because I became akin to a brain in a jar for days on end. There was no physical pain and no real awareness of anything around me. Except for a few fleet-ing moments that I cannot forget. When somebody screws bolts into your forehead, for example, you are required to remain conscious. With a hangman's fracture of my C2 vertebra, I was required to do just that.

'OK, Michael, I'm just going to apply some pressure on your forehead now. This might feel a little strange but it's quite normal.' And with that a man started to twist a screw into my skull.

Grind your teeth together slowly enough to shake your head – that's how it felt, probably because that's how it was. Then the torque screwdriver went 'ping', presumably to ensure it didn't continue to screw through my skull and into my brain. That remains a vivid memory, and I have the scars to prove it.

Then I thought I was being molested: 'What the *fuck* are you doing?'

'Nothing to worry about, it's all OK. I'm just inserting a catheter.'

'Oh, right.' I had *no* idea what a catheter was. Through embarrassment I said nothing else, and for quite a while I became worried that I'd allowed a man to fiddle with me. I wanted my mum so badly at that point.

Mick was the first person I saw after coming out of theatre. He lived in Lambourn back then, fifty miles closer than Mum was in Southampton. I'll never forget his first words to me, but I ought to give you some background as to why he delivered them.

I'd yet to try ecstasy, but it seemed that most young people had by 1995. So much so that by that spring Ken and Deirdre Barlow had staged a bedside vigil next to their daughter Tracy in *Coronation Street*'s latest dramatic plot. Tracy had been in a coma for quite some time after taking an ecstasy pill and viewers had been on tenterhooks as to whether or not she'd pull through after her ill-advised descent into decadent drug abuse. By all accounts, Mick had been left to stew on that plotline scenario and imagine that my own bizarre hospital visit was in some way connected to the nightlife enjoyed by Ken and Deirdre's daughter. To add insult to injury, Mick also had to wait, like everyone else, until I came through my operation.

Personally, I felt fine. Not for a minute did I think that I was in any danger. Not once. I'm not a spiritual person, and it might have been the medication, but, apart from the embarrassment, I knew I was going to be all right. Granted, I felt rather stupid and very ashamed, but morphine genuinely aids your booze fear.

Little did I know that Mum and Dad had been told that my lung bleed was so severe that I was given a 50–50 chance of making it through the night because I was losing more fluid than they could replace.

I was lying flat on a bed when Mick loomed into view above me, silhouetting his head in front of another fluorescent strip light.

'All right?' He might have gripped my hand. He was clearly trying hard and there was a brief pause because I was a bit fucked up. I certainly couldn't nod because I'd just had a halo neck brace screwed into my head. Therefore he spoke as if *he* were the victim in this bizarre series of events: 'I've been waiting here for fucking ages! Nobody would tell me what was going on!'

'Yeah?' was all I could manage. I was a bit tired.

'Yeah! I've been in this fucking hospital for that long now. I feel like Ken Fucking Barlow!'

People came and went. I cried when I saw my mum, and she told me what a catheter was for. That made me feel a lot better.

My best mate, Jim Slape, arrived. He fainted at the sight of me and woke up in a hospital bed in a ward down from intensive care. They gave him a banana.

My Grandad Jack also arrived. He too fainted at the sight of me and woke up in a hospital bed in a ward down from intensive care. They gave him a banana as well.

'When you get out of here, I'm going to take you down to the Malt Shovel and get you proper pissed!' he said when I next saw him. He was standing there crying in his paisley tie and green cardigan. Grandma tried to tell me how they'd had a puncture on the way.

Pughie, Richard and Andy arrived along with a few of the football lads. They hung a four pack of lager on the drip hook above me.

A television was brought in and a mirror was angled above me so that I could watch Nayim score from the halfway line as Real Zaragoza beat Arsenal in the Cup Winners' Cup final. I've seen it since and it still doesn't seem right. I thought he hit it left-footed.

Phil arrived with his best mate Bob Charles, a former Saints goalkeeper who supplied the whole family with a string of ropey second-hand cars, on the day that they first tried to tilt my bed upright. I vomited quite remarkably. Not a sympathetic visit that one, as 'Honest Bob' blamed me for making him feel unwell.

My girlfriend Anna was there throughout. She was always there. Through all the worry, confusion, madness, the friends and family – kindness personified. I still love her for it.

A nurse called Ros was the leading light on that ward in the Bristol Royal Infirmary and a major angel – harsh, kind and fair all at the same time.

'I don't want to talk to anyone,' I protested.

'This is a phone call you'll have to take. I don't care how grumpy you are, you're going to reception.' Three nurses, plus Anna navigated the ward's corridor and positioned my bed next to the reception desk. The phone was handed to me. I was looking at another fluorescent strip light. It was a Sunday, about lunchtime.

'Hello?' I said.

'Now then! What have you got yourself into? We've got a big game today and you've got yourself into a right state!' Bally was laughing.

'Sorry, boss, I think I've failed a fitness test today.' I smiled for the first time in ages.

'Don't worry, son, we'll be all right without you, I'm sure!' I smiled and I will never forget looking at Anna. She clearly knew all about this.

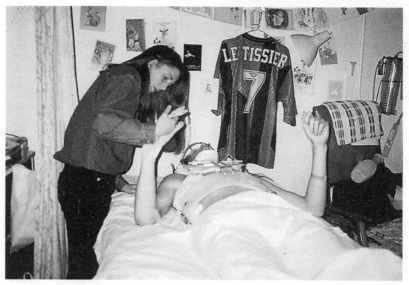

My girlfriend Anna picking up the pieces

'Good luck, boss!' I said. I was getting a bit blubbery by that stage.

'Hang on!' said Bally. 'I've got someone else who wants to speak to you.' I could hear him handing the phone over.

'Michael?'

'Yeah?'

'It's Matt.'

'Hello, Matt,' I was overwhelmed by now. Not by the emotions of speaking to Matthew Le Tissier but by the kindness and the thought that had obviously gone into it. 'We'll win this for you today, mate.'

'I hope you do, mate. Get a goal for me!'

'I will.' It was getting awkward by now, he handed me back to Alan.

'Alright, son? We've got to get on but we're all thinking of you. Love you lots.'

'Love you too, boss.'

I always thought they won that day. I remember being told that Le Tissier had scored the second against Leicester at the Dell to put Saints 2–0 up, and at that point I must have fallen asleep. It was the last game of the season and I knew we were playing Leicester because all of the playing staff were given a fixture list at the start of the season. A lot had happened in the last ten months, and not many of my dreams had come true. On top of that, morphine-induced constipation makes emotional depression feel like a holiday camp when you've broken half of your skeleton. Only writing this now have I Googled the date of that Leicester match in order to find out when that phone call took place.

Saints were 2–0 up when Tiss scored. They ended up drawing 2–2.

The bastards.

THE BRIDGE AT ARNHEM

THURSDAY 6 AUGUST 2015

Life can be easy at times and, once you've got it sussed, you feel as though it'll go on for ever. It doesn't, of course, but I *feel* like it could after a brilliant week in the aftermath of Glorious Goodwood.

There was the weekend of cricket and drinking for a kick-off. It was more of a 50–50 split if I'm honest, as the fiercely contested 'Lacklustre Shield' match took place at West Ilsley on Sunday 2 August. It's an annual meeting between the Liverpool John Moores University and Granada TV Select XI and the Vile Hun XI – catchy team names, I think you'll agree. It's basically a load of my former university friends and work colleagues playing against anyone else I know in the typecast pantomime villains of the Vile Hun XI. Obviously, I'm captain of the LJMU & GTV Select XI, while my best friend from school Jim Slape skippers 'the Hun', unbeaten for the previous two years and red hot favourites to take the 2015 renewal. I told you that things were on a roll, though, and the LJMU & GTV boys prevailed in a thrilling match that was as exciting as it was drink-fuelled. As a result, I can barely provide any match details aside from the fact that I was dismissed for nought courtesy of a horrific LBW verdict by an umpire who also happened to be one of my teammates. The fact that his 14-year-

The Lacklustre Shield winners of 2015

old son was bowling for the opposition still stirs deep feelings of resentment, so much so that neither of them will receive a name-check in this book. They both disgust me.

It was one of those summer days that you just can't beat: great weather, great fun and a victory for the underdogs. The Jaadu money covered most of the costs, including the bouncy castle. We had a pirate's galleon this year.

The following day saw Harlequin Rock win at Nottingham after a string of woeful performances had made his debut season one of distinct disappointment up to that point. He'd looked bang average until we had him gelded a month ago, and I can only guess that his testicles weighed three stone, because that's how much he improved when he came back into full work again. I had another bet and he hosed up under John Egan at 8/1. I needed the money as well, because Southampton were playing

Vitesse Arnhem away in a Europa League qualifier later in the week and I would be in attendance.

I left with our racing secretary Ross Potter and my cousin Neil 'Two Sheds' Channon on the Tuesday evening. Neil's called Two Sheds because he's got two sheds in his back garden. *Two Sheds*! He's the flash Channon in the family; he's even got tattoos. He did well, though, because he organised our transport for the trip to Holland, and I can safely say that he converted me to motor-homing. I'm serious, if you've never been away in a motorhome then you don't know what you're missing. A Fiat 'Ace Milano' it was and I couldn't have been happier; I drove down to the Channel Tunnel, had a kip in the Milano on the train, and woke up with Two Sheds at the wheel on Wednesday morning halfway through Belgium. There was a case of Stella in the back for good measure, and I lounged on a luxurious bed and watched the countryside go by. There's *loads* of ragwort along the roadsides of Belgium – Holland as well. Even though I was getting away from West Ilsley, seeing all that ragwort growing along the side of the motorway as we went past Brussels and into the Netherlands just made me think of my old man. Nobody cares about livestock in that part of Europe either.

'Lazy bastards!'

Motorhoming is the way to go as far as I'm concerned. We parked up at a campsite in Oosterbeek, just outside of Arnhem, ahead of a couple of days of sightseeing and the match on Thursday night. We took our bikes, what a place.

If you've not visited Arnhem, you simply must, particularly if you're into history. The failure to hold the bridge over the Rhine at Arnhem led to the breakdown of Operation Market Garden in September 1944, and the whole campaign to end the war before Christmas ultimately ended in disaster for the Allied Forces

With Ross at the bridge in Arnhem

that landed there. The personal stories of tragedy, bravery and heroism among both the soldiers and civilians during that time only hit home when you see the place.

It's softened if you get there with two mates in a motorhome, though.

We visited the bridge and then the Airborne Museum on Thursday morning, and I'll never forget the state that Two Sheds was in after realising the full horror of what had happened back in 1944. He was standing by a Sherman tank that was left behind and now stands as a reminder of the carnage that had taken place. He wasn't quite crying but he wasn't far off it. I spoke first: 'That was a bit intense, wasn't it?'

'I don't want to go to the cemetery. I lost it in there,' was all he could say.

'You'd have been dead handy round here in September '44, then,' I replied.

'What?'

'Well, you've spent an hour in a museum and you can't go on any more.'

'I just can't. God, it was horrible.'

'Neil, ten thousand troops landed here and ended up being completely surrounded for nine days. They ran out of food and ammunition, fourteen hundred were killed, six thousand captured, and what was left of them had to escape across the river any way they could.'

'Yeah, I know. *Horrible.*'

'And you're struggling with the thought of visiting the cemetery?'

We smiled.

The war cemetery brought it home even more: row upon row of headstones, the names and ages making the dead British and Polish soldiers all too real and far too young. It was busy enough, with plenty of tourists taking photographs. The mood was sombre and reflective. Ross, Neil and I stood there for quite some time. I can only describe it as lovely. It doesn't seem the right word to use but standing there, on a bright summer day it was just that.

Lovely.

A phone beeped ten feet or so away and an English bloke, middle-aged, took it out of his pocket. 'Fuck me!' he said to his friend next to him. 'Broad has taken eight for fifteen at Trent Bridge! The Aussies are all out for sixty!' We looked at each other with amazement.

'Can you *believe* that?' said Ross open-mouthed.

'I know! All out for *sixty!*' I said. I looked at Two Sheds, who was just gazing across the seemingly endless rows of headstones.

'Incredible.'

Arnhem war cemetery

I'm not sure if we were all on the same page at that moment.

With the Ashes series going our way at home, Saints kept the winning theme on track with an easy victory over Vitesse Arnhem that night, and a truly great trip was rounded off as the Ace Milano arrived back at West Ilsley Stables the following evening. Nancy From Nairobi had just completed a double for us by winning at Newmarket under Silvestre de Sousa, with John Egan having ridden Sixties Pilgrim to victory earlier on the card. I'm in the house right now and reflecting on the week just past. Glorious Goodwood, playing cricket and a few days in Arnhem had given me three things: fun, friends and context.

One of our owners, John Breslin, once said to me, 'Michael, having humility doesn't mean you think less of yourself, it just means that you think of yourself less often.' We were in a Chinese in London when he said that, and I just nodded at the time because we were all a bit pissed. I remember the words, though, because he had a Glaswegian accent that made it easy to recall; it was the rhythm of his words. I know now what he meant. Just a few weeks ago I was utterly depressed and completely miserable about horses not winning races. And now I'd grabbed some context and a bit of humility while having a laugh along the way. He was a wise man, John Breslin.

'I'VE SOMETHING TO TELL YOU'

MONDAY 10 AUGUST 2015

We'd finished second lot this morning and were heading up the driveway of West Ilsley Stables on the way to the gallops to see third lot exercise. A typical Monday morning with horses fresh, well and causing worry. Good spirits, though – even the old man, until he turned to me and said, 'I've something to tell you.'

'What?' I asked, unconcerned until he sighed deeply.

'I've got to go in for an op.'

'What? An operation?'

'Well, they've found a growth on my intestines. It's not cancerous as such and they're not worried about it. I've been having all those tests after that night in hospital and, you know, well, they could leave it in there and just monitor it, but I don't want to fuck about and they agree.'

'When is it?'

'They aren't too bothered, they said I can fit it in when it suits me. I don't want it getting in the way of the sales, so we'll slot it in as and when.'

'As and when?'

'Yeah. Look, it's nothing too serious, but serious enough to need an operation. Don't worry yourself about it.'

'OK.'

That was it, really. I won't worry myself about it.

Yet.

If I've learnt anything it's that Mick doesn't do details, like he doesn't really do conversation. He says what he thinks, you go along with it, and that's the end of the matter. I'll have to chip away for information little and often. I'll have to play the long game here, because there's no other real alternative. Sure, we spend seven days a week in each other's company, but don't think that is any reason to think we really have each other's ear. Just because we go down the pub doesn't mean that I really know what's going on in his head. We share subjects, but you'd never describe them as conversations. They are usually kicked off with one of his sweeping criticisms. Here's one on cricket: 'That Joe Root – he's weak as piss.'

'What do you mean? He's averaged over eighty in the calendar year.'

'Yeah, but you can hardly describe the West Indies as any good, can you?'

'But he's just scored a century, a half-century in Cardiff and another at Trent Bridge against the Aussies.'

'Yeah, but he was hopeless against them at Lords and, let's face it, Australia were crap in the other Tests – *Root is as weak as piss.*'

That's the end of matters.

That's also the way with most fathers and sons of our age. I know what he's *like*, but it's difficult to *know* him. And that's not a plea for more understanding from him, or any real source of regret. It's just what he's like. It's laughable, really, and something that will never change. 'I've got to go in for an op' demands as much detail and discussion as 'Joe Root is weak as piss'. One statement is true, the other isn't. I'm already starting to worry.

As we returned from the gallops and parked the wagon outside the office he spoke again: 'Look, it isn't good, but it's all under control. I've had so many tests you wouldn't believe it, but they know what they're doing. All we've got to do for now is keep the mixer going. They are flying at the minute but we can't let up. We need fucking winners. For now, *that's all that matters*.'

THE VOLLEY

MANSEL JUNIORS, BAKERS DROVE, 1984 – 85

It's a wasteland now. I drove past it the other day. A sad, neglected relic with so many memories: Bakers Drove, the home of Mansel Juniors, a place where I'd sometimes score five in a 7–0 drubbing of Langley Manor or Hedge End Rangers or Warsash Wasps, while I'd sulk like the spoilt brat I was and blame everyone else as Windsor United battered us 11–1.

The Southampton and District Tyro League in the mid-1980s. Bakers Drove was, and still is, in Rownhams in Southampton, not exactly a salubrious area of one of the nation's most famous port cities. A dockers' town, one that I'm still very proud of, and have become even more affectionate about the longer I've lived away from it. I love Southampton. I love the way I know the areas, the talk and the codes people use to sum up certain individuals, blatantly obvious scenarios and local dialect: 'he's a bit Flower Roads'; 'it all went a bit Townhill Park after that'; 'the nipper don't know what I mean, mush'.

By the age of ten, after ridding myself of my obsession with Joe Corrigan, I no longer wanted to be Manchester City's goalkeeper. I'd decided that I was going to captain Saints and score the winner in the FA Cup final at Wembley like Bobby had. I'd even worked out in my head that I could achieve this goal by 1990 if the breaks came my way and if Lawrie McMenemy wasn't so blind that he couldn't realise what a threat I'd be up front alongside Steve Moran.

Times move on, though, and a year on from the stellar season that I've yet to describe to you at Mansel Juniors, both Moran (to Leicester City, a crying shame) and McMenemy (to Sunderland, what was he thinking?) had left the Dell. That meant that further down the road I'd have to catch the eye of the new manager, Chris Nicholl and usurp Jimmy Case as skipper to lift the Cup on that balmy May afternoon at the start of a new decade. Not for the first time was my imagination, my ambition and, let's be frank, my abysmal maths woefully inaccurate (who captains the Cup winners at the age of seventeen?), but in 1984–85 my short-falls as a footballer were put brutally into perspective as well.

Guess who by.

As with the fathers' race at the Atherley School's sports day just a few years beforehand, Mick was on hand to watch me play a game for Mansel Juniors at Bakers Drove. While Nicky's sports day was a unique occasion, I'd play football every Sunday morning, and Mick would often turn up to watch me playing with his mates before having a few pints when we got home in the afternoon.

Kids in the mid-1980s could handle any weather. Even the substitutes, those kids so hopeless they couldn't get a game on a Sunday morning, wore acrylic tracksuit tops that wouldn't warm a budgie. The day I remember above all others was cold. Freez-ing cold. A classic scene from the 1980s was being played out. Parents were shouting at the referee, hurling insults at the oppo-sition's parents along the touchline, and occasionally employing verbal abuse at a ten-year-old child attempting to take a throw in – it was a home game at Bakers Drove, after all.

Mick always stood on the right wing, where I always seemed to end up getting the ball. He would never shout at me. He told me to just ignore everyone else and to get my 'heels to the line and have a go at them'. I loved him watching me play. Mick was never a shouty parent. He was barely a parent, if I can type that without making it sound barbed. He was just 'my dad'. He never preached, never smacked me, never sent me to bed with a thick ear and seldom resorted to discipline. He was seldom home.

When he was, I'd drag him into the back garden. He had a pair of blue-striped Patrick trainers that he wore while he set about perfecting my first touch on the lawn, improving my forward defence against his awful leg spin, weaning yearlings and mucking out the horses. He encouraged me in a unique way in those Patrick trainers: '*Get hold of the fucking thing!* If you've got it, you can do something with it – if you can't get hold of it, you've got no chance of doing anything with it!' That was all he ever did – kick it at me at awkward angles. It was all about your first touch.

The game at Bakers Drove was locked at 2–2 against a team I can't remember with only minutes remaining, and our goalie was a big lad who was good at kicking it out of his hands. That was our main tactic, actually. I was standing near the halfway line when he kicked it downfield. I remember it coming straight towards me, a Mitre Multiplex size 4. Nobody wanted to head those in under-11s football – nobody would today, in fact, they were harder than a dog's head – so I just did what I was told to do in the garden at home: I got hold of the fucking thing. I intended to stop it dead and pass it sideways but, instead, it popped up over my right shoulder and I had to use my left foot. I just swivelled, and I even had a look before smashing it on the volley towards the right wing like I was Glenn Hoddle. The ball landed by Richard Kenway's feet, just in front of my dad. Richard then crossed it, but there was nobody to finish off a sublime piece of football created by a ten-year-old boy. I was that little boy.

I remember getting in the car. It was Mick's green Mercedes, a car that straddled our lives from the end of the Manchester City days and well into his time at Norwich City, who he was playing for by then. That green Merc had done a lot of miles. I was muddy and cold, with my Patrick boots and Kevin Keegan shinpads still on and the acrylic Mansel Juniors tracksuit top with the sponsors logo of 'Botley Roofing'. I got in the passenger seat, ready for the praise.

'I'll never have a go at you again,' he said. 'But what you did out there was crap.'

Now, if I were to say that I was confused, it would be an understatement. Did he not see the volley?

'You got bullied by those two in the middle and all you could do was try to look clever. They aren't half the player you are between them, but you did nothing to try to change that.'

There were twin brothers playing against me that day. They had blond hair. I thought I deserved more than I was getting, but the old man just kept digging at me like a schoolteacher who didn't want to get angry: 'You just fucked around and waited for the ball to come to you. You did *nothing* about those two, you just waited for your turn. That doesn't mean you're any good at football. That means you're spoilt and lazy. You could have scored the winner if you'd wanted to.' His voice was kind – I bet that comes as a shock. I think this was him trying to provide advice and encouragement. He wasn't very good at it. I was sinking into the green Merc's passenger seat, and welling up inside. He wasn't a cruel dad – all he'd ever done up until that point was praise me – but that was a horrible drive home. We were driving through the innumerable roundabouts in Townhill Park.

'You did something today that I would never have been able to do. You've got more talent than I ever had at your age, but once you hit that ball you just stood there and thought about how good it was. *It was fucking brilliant by the way!* But if you want to be any good, you'd better start to sharpen up, because that wasn't the end of the game there and then. You've got to be there at the death knocking the fucking thing in the goal! It's about winning, not fucking standing there thinking you're good.'

I cried. A lot.

Worst thing was, he was right. You don't have to look good doing it – people who get to the top in anything don't stand about rating their performances. They get results in any way they can. As he said after telling me about needing the operation when we pulled up in the wagon: 'We need fucking winners, that's all that matters.'

UNCLE JOHN

FRIDAY 14 AUGUST 2015

We'd just finished a work morning and were all heading off home for a quick change before an afternoon at Newbury. It's our local track and we'd had a good morning with the horses really starting to thrive. Then the phone rang. It was Grandma, telling us that Uncle John and Thelma were going home and wanted to say goodbye. They'd been staying in Grandma's bungalow. She's been there since moving in with Grandad Jack back in 2000. It's sad to think that Jack lasted little more than a year from then because he was happy here, plonked on the estate like a proper country gent, not that he spoke like or indeed acted anything like the sort. He did get a tweed jacket, though, and it would have been interesting to see how his wardrobe might have escalated in that direction had he lasted a few more years.

Grandma is happy slap bang in the middle of all the staff accommodation, surrounded by families, only a hundred yards from the office. Her sister, Auntie Crid, is a regular visitor although her baby brother John a little less so. You'll remember Uncle John from his forceful entry to the Intensive Care Unit at Nottingham University. If you recall, I'd first met Uncle John in the week after Jack died, when he arrived with Auntie Thelma in his caravan and set about threatening the staff. He's a very

rare visitor, but I like him immensely. He's good company, with
a million tales to tell, most of them beginning with the phrase,
'A while back . . .'

'A while back' in John's world can refer to an incident that
occurred anywhere between two weeks and twenty years ago.
I like that.

I'll be honest, I didn't even know John and Thelma were here this
week, but Mick and I made our way up to Grandma's to be confronted by the ever-spirited Uncle John in the kitchen. He's immediately familiar, swears like a trooper and remains utterly forthright
in everything he says. He reminds me of someone else in my family.
Mick decided to get the ball rolling: 'Any news for us then, John?'
'Not really, boy. Went to Robert's funeral a while back. Dad's
brother's lad's son – your cousin.' This took us some while to work
out. 'Do you remember Robert, Mike?' (He calls Mick 'Mike' –
always has.)

'Not really.'

'Yes you do! Robert! Only a year younger than you.'

'Oh, *Robert!*' I knew he had no recollection. 'What happened
to him, then?'

'He had a row with his next-door neighbour.'

'Heart attack?' Mick guessed. It seemed like a logical
assumption.

'No. He got hit with a shovel.'

I interjected: '*He got hit with a shovel?*'

'Oh yeah.'

'So that killed him?' I asked incredulously. It seemed like
a reasonable question.

'Oh no! He went into the house, came back out with a gun and
shot his neighbour.'

'*He shot his neighbour?*'

Both Mick and I were stood, gobsmacked, leaning against Grandma's sideboard. John just ploughed on: 'Yeah.'

'*Dead?*'

'Yeah, dead.'

At this point I noticed John's surprise that we thought it was surprising that our family had had a murderer in its ranks.

'So why did you go to *Robert's* funeral if he was the one who shot his neighbour?' Mick asked.

'Oh, he topped himself in the nick.'

I'd like to say that Uncle John's news ended there, but for some reason I asked another question in order to change the subject and kill the sense of bemusement in Grandma's kitchen: 'So, you're staying out of trouble, though?'

'Well, more or less.'

'What do you mean "more or less"?'

'Well, I had a bit of trouble on the motorway a while back, trying to overtake a young kid. He didn't like it and started to race us. Anyway, we pulled over, and as I was getting out of the car he hit me. My glasses fell off and everything.' 'So what did you do?' asked Mick, who was looking more at me than he was at John by this stage. 'Well, I couldn't exactly find my glasses there and then because he was threatening me, so I sort of knew where he was and connected with a couple round his head and got a couple into his ribs. When he was on the ground I managed to get a boot into him as well. Then I found my glasses.'

This is exactly what Uncle John is like.

'What happened then?' I asked.

'Well, he said he wouldn't press charges, didn't he, John?' interjected Auntie Thelma.

'*What!?*' Mick's features were a mixture of visible shock and incredulity.

'Well, the police visited him in hospital and I think he was a bit embarrassed – me being eighty-five and him being twenty-two and that,' added John.

'You put a twenty-two-year old in hospital!?' I asked.

'Yeah! He hit me and I lost my glasses.'

I looked at Grandma, who was nodding along throughout. All she said was, 'What is he like?'

Mick gestured me towards the door.

'See ya later, John,' was all I could come up with.

'Yeah, see ya, John,' said Mick, shaking his head. 'See ya, boy.'

As we walked down the path of Grandma's bungalow I whispered out of the side of my mouth to the old man: 'Is any of that likely to be true?'

'I wouldn't put it past him. He's always been as mad as a fucking hatter.'

We had a great day at Newbury, one completely at odds with the bizarre morning with Uncle John and the building trepidation ahead of Mick's operation. Czabo and Silvestre de Sousa, although unfancied, took the fillies' maiden before Epsom Icon won the Listed Denford Stud Stakes to really grab the limelight. She's just become a valuable asset, Mick was on Channel 4 again, and although I suppose the fortunes of our horses could have featured far more prominently in this chapter, the chat with Uncle John in my grandma's kitchen has dominated my thoughts today.

TAPLIN'S DELIGHT

MONDAY 24 AUGUST 2015

Silly, really, but today was a very good one. And then a bad one. Despite having a winner.

Peter Taplin and Sue Bunny tipped up to see their horses this morning. The last time we were all together was the morning before Mick and I visited the John Radcliffe Hospital and the start of our current stresses amid an upturn in fortunes on the racecourse. I like Peter Taplin immensely. He was one of Mick's first owners, one of his longest-standing mates. He's a man of few words but very loyal, very kind and genuine to a fault. Sue is similar. Although she's only been involved in horses with us for three years, I already know she's a proper person. I knew so immediately – kind, caring and, most importantly of all, very trusting. You can do your job so much more effectively when somebody believes in you. Shit, you can live your life more effectively under those conditions.

Mick waddled off home after we were done with the horses while I took Pete and Sue to see the yearling fillies that are about to come in for breaking and pre-training on the new land at West Ilsley. Then we went to the Swan in East Ilsley for a bit of lunch. To our surprise, the place was packed with elderly folk on one of their monthly Macmillan Cancer Support coffee mornings.

We arrived at the arse end of that, but not too late to invest in a few raffle tickets – all for a good cause. We weren't aware that we were about to be cast as villains on their day out, though.

All three of us threw a tenner in for the raffle tickets and had a stab at guessing how many hundreds and thousands were on the magnificent cake in the bar, before ordering a round of drinks and a bit of grub. This wasn't viewed, however, as the kind, charitable act that I thought it might be. A minibus of pensioners doesn't have ten pounds each to blow on raffle tickets. They spend little more than a pound on one strip and while there were ten or fifteen of them there, this meant that Pete, Sue and I had monopolised the raffle-ticket market to the tune of about 85 per cent. As a result, Pete enjoyed a six-timer – even better than the day Middler and I enjoyed our five-timer on that Thursday a couple of years ago, although Pete's odds of success weren't exactly 54,000/1. In very quick succession he won four cans of Guinness, a box of bathroom lotions, a bottle of Scotch, a bottle of white wine, a tin of chocolate biscuits and a cake, barely sitting down after picking up one prize before having to return to get the next. After he picked up the bottle of Scotch, he just said, 'I might as well just wait here, hadn't I?'

The landlord of the pub pulled out the next ticket: 'Pink ticket: 257!'

'Yep, that's mine,' said Pete, before returning to our table with the Scotch and wine.

Things were getting a little hostile by then. The pensioners were grumbling and you could quite clearly hear their utterances of disappointment and disgust: 'Just look at the tickets they've got between them. They've bought the whole lot!'

'I know. I don't know if they think they're clever, but this is just silly.'

Taplin the raffle king

'You're right there. Still, if that's what makes them happy, let them get on with it, I say.'

The elderly tend to speak slightly louder than they think they are. Sue was crying in hysterics while also glowing red with embarrassment. Pete cared not a jot. Just after Pete had swept the board in the raffle, the landlord then announced the winner of who had guessed, to the nearest sprinkle, the number of hundreds and thousands on top of the enormous cake situated in pride of place by the bar: 'And the winner of the prize cake, with a guess of 327 is . . . Peter Taplin!'

'Of course it is,' said Pete, as he ambled up to collect his latest prize.

The minibus pensioners shot daggers at him. I almost fell off my chair. Pete and Sue have decided on the name of their next horse together. They're going to call it Raffle King.

After lunch, I returned home, showered and changed before heading off to an evening meeting at Leicester races.

Unilit won again, marking herself out as an improving filly who was giving her owners in the Insignia syndicate an awful lot of fun, but it was a young gelding called Gandvik, who runs for our Lord Ilsley syndicate, who was giving me the most cause for concern.

Gandvik ran for the first time at Bath back in May. When I say that he 'ran', what I mean is that he finished eighth of nine runners and nearly snapped in half. He returned home so sore and so lame as a result of the firm ground that he had a month of box rest to get over what was a less than enjoyable experience for him on his racecourse debut. We got him going again towards the end of June, and he was the same as he'd been since he'd arrived from the sales back in November: he was *willing*. He tried so hard in everything he did and he clearly relished the job that he was bred for. Gandvik's only problem was the fact that his legs didn't necessarily combine to make him what you'd call a perfect mover. He moved like a garden rotavator, in fact. He has plenty of talent, though, which has always been abundantly clear because, in spite of his flaws, he's able to work with the majority of our horses at home on the gallops. He's that bad a mover that you don't want to watch. He runs like a clown on stilts, with little or no fluidity in his action, meaning that he runs from the shoulder, with his knees and fetlock joints doing very little to cushion the blow as he stretches every sinew to cover the ground ahead of him. It's horrible.

Tonight, on his fourth run at Leicester, he finished third of 13 runners in a maiden race. What I saw this evening increased my respect for the thoroughbred racehorse tenfold. Silvestre de Sousa nearly fell off him twice. Gandvik tried so hard that he almost threw his legs off while Silvestre urged him on as they entered the final two furlongs. He was pitching and pivoting over his forelegs like a camel, yet sticking his neck out bravely as his syndicate members cheered him on. I just shivered, though. This is not the sort of action that will see Gandvik last too long. Just after the two pole, Silvestre gave him a crack with his stick and the horse responded immediately before stumbling, Silvestre almost losing his right foot in the stirrups. Having regained his balance, Silvestre found that Gandvik was still carrying him along, so he pulled his whip through to his left hand and, with a willing accomplice beneath him, gave him another crack. Again the horse stuck his neck out but again he pitched and again Silvestre nearly lost his feet in the irons.

All around me the syndicate were growing in both volume and excitement: 'Go on Gandvik! Go on Silvestre!'

I wasn't one of them. All I was thinking was, 'Please stop trying, you daft fucker. You'll kill yourself.'

It was an astonishing run – a herculean effort from a young horse who only wants to please. Trouble is, he might be the most stupid animal in history. You certainly can't force a horse to do anything it doesn't want to do, but tonight, for the first time ever, I wanted a horse to not do something that everyone else wanted him to do.

Gandvik clearly loves racing and he clearly has ability, but I've seen enough bad movers to realise that they'll meet with disaster at some stage, usually through wear and tear and repetitive-strain injuries. Gandvik, though, looks liable to snap in half at any moment. That's not a repetitive-strain injury – he's only two.

With Gandvik and his famous front legs

Gandvik's enthusiastic owners greeted Silvestre when he unsad-
dled and gave his assessment: 'You're right, he's not the greatest
mover, is he? He couldn't handle the track and I nearly fell off a
couple of times. But the thing is, he kept taking me forward.'

'What would you do with him?' I said.

'I don't know. What about trying the all-weather?'

'Would you want to run him round a bend then?' I asked.

Silvestre gave me the look of a rider who is well on course to becoming this year's champion jockey and just shrugged.

'Perhaps you could try it?'

The look Silvestre gave me left me in no doubt as to what he was implying: *we* could try running Gandvik around a bend on the all-weather, but *he* wouldn't be riding him.

I couldn't blame him.

On the way home I called the old man. He was in bed.

'Did you see that?'

'Yeah. It wasn't pretty, was it?'

'Wasn't pretty, Dad? It was fucking horrific!'

'I don't know what we can do with the little horse,' said the old man. 'He certainly wants to do it.'

'I know, but I'll be with the syndicate when he breaks down. You know it's going to happen. Christ, at least some part of this game should be fun, and that was horrible. Why doesn't the horse just stop?'

'I don't know. He's a tough bugger, I'll give him that, but I think you're right. I've seen some bad movers in my time but nothing as bad as him. We'll see how he is in the morning, but if he's jarred up again he'll have to go and do something else. Anyway, well done with the winner. I'll see you in the morning. A big day ahead.'

Tomorrow is indeed a big day. Malabar is working ahead of a trip to run in New York. Not only that, but Mick has scheduled this crucial workout ahead of a stay in Swindon tomorrow afternoon.

He's going in for the operation.

THE SHALBOURNE SUITE

GREAT WESTERN HOSPITAL, SWINDON, TUESDAY 25 AUGUST 2015

A busy work morning saw us put the finishing touches to Malabar's preparation for the Sands Point Stakes at Belmont Park, New York, on 12 September. She's thrived since winning at Goodwood last month, and went very well over seven furlongs on the summer ground at West Ilsley. With that done, Mick could then concentrate on the other matter at hand. He was due at Swindon hospital at one o'clock before being operated on this evening.

We've sort of had a chat about things here and there, danced around the subject a fair bit, barely spoken in any detail, and filled in the awkward gaps by talking about horses, football and cricket up until this point. While driving back from the gallops having overseen third lot, however, he turned to me and said, 'Right, if the worst is to happen, you know, today, and things went wrong, you'll have to take things on.' I sat there thinking that this could have been handled a little better. I awaited something profound and emotional, something he'd perhaps been rehearsing alone as he contemplated his own mortality. That's not quite what came out though: 'Just remember this. There's always stock on the ground, get yourself out and about, because you never know where a good horse can come from.'

That was it.

We've all been sworn to secrecy, with only Gill Hedley in the office and close family aware that Mick was going to hospital for an operation, bar one: Grandma. Again, I couldn't help feeling that a more up-front and rational approach to the process might have been more appropriate going forward, but it was Mick's call so I didn't bother saying anything. He'd broken the news to everyone by phone. Grandma had been fetched by his brother Phil to spend a few days in Bishop's Waltham for the weekend, with the plan being to say nothing to her until Mick was back home. I wasn't too sure as to what he'd told them all, but I very much doubted that he had the necessary communication skills to paint them an accurate picture of what was really going on. I work with him every day, and all I really knew was that he had a blockage in his intestines that needed removing. It was nothing more, nothing less, apparently: 'Obviously, it's not a fucking good thing but it's not cancer, or anything that will require chemotherapy, or anything like that. We've just got to lie low for a month or so and then we'll be up and running again. You know what you're doing here, and I'll be home in a couple or three days.'

I had pushed for a little more information from him, but digging deeper led to less and less detail. I'd have had better luck discussing Joe Root's batting average. 'What about telling Keith and putting him straight?' I asked. Keith Evans is Mick's assistant in the yard. He knows every horse, every joint and every leg of every animal under his care. A crucial part of the business, and if not irreplaceable then he's certainly the next best thing to it. I just thought it would make sense if he were in the know.

'I'll speak to Keith about it, yeah.'

'What about the owners? What should I say to them?'

'I'll speak to the ones who need to know. Patrick and Pete

know already, and I'll get hold of the Aisbitts as well. They need to know how Malabar went this morning anyway.'

As ever, he wasn't helping me. Just a tiny glimpse into his mind would have been helpful, because the only concrete instruction I had to fall back on was to look at plenty of blood-stock, because you never know where a good horse can come from. Useful, but that was all I had as guidance if he died on the operating table.

That and the fact that he didn't want a fuss made, because, *'You should never show any weakness to any fucker. Ever.'*

Terrific.

I found him in the house just before he set off at midday and collared him on the Keith issue.

'I'll phone him now. Where's the phone?'

I fetched the phone, dialled Keith's number and handed it over.

'Keith! Yeah, it's me. Listen, I've got to go into hospital for an operation. Shouldn't take more than a couple of days at the most. I'll leave it to you and Michael to sort out between you. You know what you're doing, all right? Good. Bye.' He put down the receiver. 'Right, that's him done. Come on, darling, we'd best get off . . .'

He dropped into the office about fifteen minutes later with Jill to check that Malabar's travel plans were all in order: the horse-box to Antwerp via the ferry with Lesley, our travelling head lass, and then a flight to JFK where our head lad Jon Dennis would be waiting for her, to transfer her to quarantine quarters at Belmont Park racecourse. We still hadn't confirmed a jockey booking because Silvestre de Sousa had commitments at home, so we'd have to go for an American jockey. It's been bloody hard to pin one down as well.

Mick sped off in the car with Jill. I was to join them later before he went down for the op. Gill Hedley then informed Ross in the office as to what was going on without revealing the full details: 'A couple of days, nothing to worry about, just field his calls, deal with what you can yourself and then say that he'll be in touch.' As Ross was trying to take it all in, I had the sudden urge to add, 'And don't show any weakness to any fucker. *Ever.*' But I didn't. I went home and made a sandwich.

I left home at one o'clock. 'Two Sheds' phoned as I was making my way to Swindon: 'All right? How are you?' Unusually, his voice was full of grave concern.

'I'm all right! What's happening?' I was unsure as to what he knew. He obviously knew more than I did because his dad had obviously relayed the news that he'd heard from his brother. Mick and Phil aren't the greatest of communicators individually, so obviously they'd made a bit of a bollocks of matters by the time the 'details' had reached my cousin. He continued, 'Your dad. This whole cancer thing. Are you OK?'

'Cancer?'

'Yeah, that's what my dad said. Cancer.'

'That's the first I've heard about it. What else do you know?'

'Just that Mick's got cancer and he's gone in to have it removed.'

I was stunned that I didn't know. Mick just told me it was 'gunk', a blockage that needed to be removed. I'd put it down to the anti-inflammatories that he'd been shovelling down to keep the pain of his arthritis at bay for the past twenty years. I couldn't believe he had cancer.

'Well, that's what Phil told me,' was all Two Sheds said.

I went through the actual information I'd been given by the old man: *It's nothing, no actual cancer, just a blockage. Serious, but not that serious, and that it certainly wasn't fucking cancer.*

It may seem odd but we both broke out with laughter. We both know how seriously bizarre any important news being broken by Mick to Phil (or vice versa for that matter) would have been. Clearly, Mick delivering serious news to Phil hadn't gone terribly well. It must be hard to break news that you're ill and need surgery to your younger brother without showing any weakness. We finished our call and I immediately phoned Jill. She answered and I didn't mess about: 'Has he got cancer?'

'What?'

'I've just had Neil on and he was asking me about Mick having cancer!'

'Hang on a sec.' I sensed that she was walking out of Mick's earshot in the hospital. 'Right, it's not cancer, it's a carcinoid, which does sound like it's cancer but it's a relatively benign growth, if that makes sense. They know where it is and just need to remove it. Where did Neil get the idea that it was cancer?'

'Well, I presume from the conversation Mick had with Phil. If I know less than anyone else, I wouldn't mind knowing everything now.'

'Don't panic, it's not *cancer* cancer. I don't know where they got that idea from.'

I did. Certain men, of a certain age, from a certain generation are incapable of communicating anything with any clarity. That would be a sure sign of weakness. By two o'clock I arrived outside the Shalbourne Suite, a private ward attached to Swindon hospital, and I immediately saw a jump jockey's sponsored BMW with his name emblazoned on its side in the car park. I was terrified that he would see me, and that, in some way, I might show any weakness. I pulled my cap down and scurried in the direction of the entrance. I found Mick and Jill in room five, just sitting there. Waiting. He's not used to waiting.

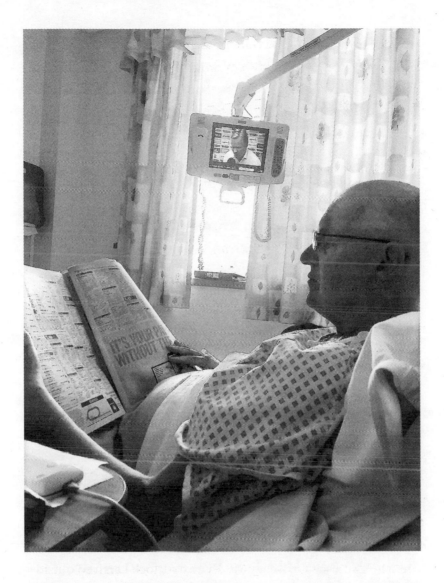

'We've been waiting here since we arrived. The anaesthetic bloke came down and he seemed happy enough and we've just been sitting here ever since. It's fucking boring in here.'

I was shocked that sitting in a hospital room waiting for an operation was a less than thrilling experience. However, with almost perfect timing, in strode a warm and friendly figure: 'Ah, there you are! Hello, Mick!'

'Hello, Jeremy. You well?'

'Yes, not too bad. Hi, Jill!'

I was sitting in the corner by the door and hadn't been noticed. Mick did the introduction: 'That's my lad, Jack – I mean Michael, sorry, that's Michael.'

'Hello, Michael.'

'Hello.' That's all I had, although I liked Jeremy Glass immediately.

'Right then,' the surgeon began. 'You're booked in for six o'clock, everything is in place and it's a very quick procedure. We know exactly what it is and they are very straightforward and uncomplicated. Only an hour or two, depending on what we find, but we know what we're faced with and I don't see any real problems, apart from your recovery. It will take some getting over.'

'Brilliant,' said Mick. 'I've signed all the forms and they said I won't need a bag or anything. I won't need a bag, will I?' The very thought of it obviously terrified him. A colostomy bag – the ultimate sign of weakness.

'No, not unless things are far worse than we think they are. Anyway, six o'clock! I'll see you then!'

'Righto, Jeremy. Thank you. Thank you very much.' He's seldom so polite.

And that was it. My dad, my step mum and me, sitting in a hospital room. He was right, it was quite boring, but at least the surgeon instilled some confidence in me. And so we sat there, for ages. We exchanged some of the most blatant, banal and inexcusable small talk in the history of human life – the weather, the ground at Bath, whether they've watered at Goodwood, or if we'd managed to sort out a jockey for Malabar – truly abysmal stuff. I had to get out for an hour.

'Right, I'm off to get my hair cut,' I said, as I got to my feet. 'I'll only be an hour and then you can get off Jill and I'll wait with him until he goes down.'

What a great plan, and I did need to get my hair cut. In recent years, baldness has begun to creep into the picture. That's absolutely fine, I've got no issues with that, Grandad Jack and Mick's genetics have clearly sealed my fate, but my hair has little or no idea of where to begin. Rather than just gradually envelop my entire head, I'm beginning to go bald on top and on the right side, while the left side of my head is revelling in some sort of an Indian summer. My head can't seem to get enough of growing hair on the left-hand side, absolutely loves growing hair there, in fact, while the follicles on the top and the right have sort of downed tools on me. It's not a good look. Whereas I used to go to great lengths to be trendy, instructing the barber how I wanted my hair to look, these days I just say, 'Make me look slightly less ridiculous and take as much off as you want.' And that's how I found myself getting my hair cut in Swindon at four in the afternoon.

It took me a while to find a barber's in Swindon. All I know about Swindon is that confusing bunch of roundabouts which surely represent a heavy night on acid 30 years ago at the town planners' Christmas party. I eventually tracked a place down and marched in. The act of not showing any sign of weakness *'to any fucker'* was dominating my mind by this stage of the day. I sat down and we went through the pleasantries. I explained that one side of my head grows hair and how the other side doesn't, asked for it to be levelled up a bit and told her to make it look less ridiculous.

Now, the barber's I go to in Wantage know I work in racing, they know where I work and who I work for. This place in

Swindon however had no idea who I was. They knew I wasn't a local and the very nice girl charged with the task of 'making me look less ridiculous' opened up with, 'Not seen you in here before, are you local?'

I was, by now, so fraught with paranoia that she might as well have asked, 'Your dad's obviously not too well, everyone's talking about his arrival at Swindon hospital this afternoon. He looks like he's suffering from weakness. Are you worried that it will have a long-term impact on owners sending you any horses?'

As a result, I immediately went on the defensive and things became quite absurd once we'd established I didn't live in Swindon. For some reason, I began to make up a series of lies to throw her off the scent. If I said I was from West Ilsley, she'd immediately know who I was and work out why I was there. I therefore adopted all of the lives of my best friends to make sure she wouldn't work out that I was a racehorse trainer's son visiting his father in a hospital ahead of a major operation. I started off by saying that I lived in Surrey because I have a mate called Dan who lives in Surrey.

'Married?' 'Yes.' 'Kids?' 'Yes, two – one of each.' 'What age are they at?'

At this point, unsure of the age of Dan's kids, I left Surrey. I became Stig, whose son is my godson. I know loads about Stig's kids.

'Freddie is nine and Esme is five.' 'Lovely names, what are you doing here?'

That stumped me a bit because I didn't know why I'd be in Swindon unless my dad was there for an operation. I then remembered a story that my mate Marvyn, a thespian friend from Preston, had told me concerning the time he was trying to get work experience. 'I'm an actor,' I said. I had no fucking idea where this was going but I found that I simply couldn't stop. I was even describing how I was bringing the works of Shakespeare to underprivileged kids in inner city schools when she stopped me in my tracks by mentioning that it was the summer holidays.

'I know!' I said, thinking fast in my chair, 'we're setting it all up ready for the new school year. Talk about out of the frying pan and into the fire! As soon as my two little terrors go back to school I'll be in front of a load of adolescents. Still, at least it'll open my eyes to what's in store for me!'

I'll not bore you any more but I rounded it all off by talking about the mess all kids make on the sofa and how food gets down the sides between the cushions. I was paranoid in the extreme by that stage. I told her to keep the change from a £20 note through the shame of my complete bullshit then ran out of the door and wondered whether or not I'd shown any weakness during my fifteen minutes of shame.

I returned to the Shalbourne Suite and relayed what had happened to Mick and Jill. They laughed, but clearly thought I was a bit of an idiot. To be fair, so did I. Jill was glad to leave. I don't blame her, it was a horrible situation for all of us and the small talk was quite unbearable. I sat there with my old man, and we both knew things were awkward. I'm sure there was plenty to talk about. Meaningful stuff: how we were going to work together during his recovery, the impending sales season, what this was going to mean in the following two months and how best to handle the situation that absolutely nobody other than those close to us knew about.

That, I suspect, would have been showing weakness though.

Instead, we talked about how he'd be out in a couple of days and how he'd be able to attend the Goffs' yearling sales in Ireland at the end of September. Total rubbish.

They were late in taking him down to theatre. It was almost seven before they started wheeling him out and we said goodbye. He just said, 'I'll see ya later, then.' An unnatural, forced grin on his face.

'Yeah. See ya later.'

I followed the trolley to the lift and stood by him as the doors opened. He reached out and we did this really weird American-style handshake.

And it was really weird.

'See ya.'

'See ya.'

I had a kebab on the way home.

Like the visit to the barber's, that made no sense either.

THE COFFIN DODGER

As I said at the start of this book, John Marston was my friend. He was incredibly popular and very, very funny. He was the last person I knew who'd needed an operation. He never made it out. This is what I wrote in the *West Ilsley Newsletter* after his death in April 2014:

Marsie was a top lad, a fine sportsman and a man who loved and excelled at banter. There was something of an age gap between us, about 33 years to be precise, but that didn't seem to matter. Not surprising, really, because as all of those that knew him will testify, he had a knack of rubbing along with everyone. From 'JV' in the pavilion at West Ilsley Cricket Club to the junior player he coaxed along with kindness, advice and occasional criticism, he seemed to know how to get the best out of everyone. We enjoyed a keen golf rivalry. For every time I called him the 'Coffin Dodger', he'd sink a ten-foot putt for a half, stick two fingers up and say, 'Tosser.' Every time I hit a good one, he'd stand there, deadpan, and say something far less complimentary – always with that endearing grin of his.

My biggest memory of Marsie will be laughing: with him, at him – it didn't seem to matter. He was the liveliest and brightest bloke you could meet. He always had that diary of his to hand, with a list of horses to follow and a busy and varied month ahead. Cricket, golf, horses and Kerrie dominated his plans. He always had a word of

advice that he backed up with experience. He didn't lecture, he gave
his opinions on matters that he had first-hand knowledge of.

It's only now that he's gone that I realise how much they meant. I
still have his driver and the 20p I owe him from our last game when
he won nearest the pin. How I ended up owing him money when
I'd won the match outright, I'll never know. I'll miss our Monday
afternoons at Newbury & Crookham Golf Club before I went evening
racing at Windsor. I won our 2013 season 7–5 – the first and now last
year I ever got the better of him. The saddest thing, though, is that his
presence at West Ilsley Cricket Club for what seemed set to be for ever
is at an end. One that came so quickly and will be a source of great
regret when we need runs, a spell of hand-grenade spin bowling or a
laugh and a fag. Marsie was a great friend to us all. What a lad.

I feel sorry for the word 'banter'. Poor old 'banter' has had a
hard time of things in recent years. These days it's a word widely
ridiculed, denigrated as a pastime only enjoyed by idiots. It even
has its own slang abbreviation today. 'Bantz' reduces 'banter' to
something less than worthless.

Sometimes, though, banter is all that there is. It's not shameful,
it's vitally important to men in particular, to express affection for
other men without acting as though they're soft. Because 'banter'
is cruel and funny and establishes a pecking order among peers,
regardless of whether there's an ultimate winner or not. With John
Marston and me there was never an outright winner in anything,
but I do know that there was a hell of a lot of affection that we
were both well aware of. That raised our banter to ridiculously
high levels of goading, and it was terrific fun. I miss it immensely.

Marsie was a veritable run machine in league cricket, scoring
over 12,000 runs despite the fact that he only began playing com-
petitively in his mid-thirties once his local football career came to

an end. That's what I'm told anyway, but it's easily believed. He was a total competitor and incredibly canny. I first met him when I moved down to West Ilsley from Manchester, a major change in my life, and I got involved with West Ilsley Cricket Club, mainly turning up hung over, having a few more pints to level me out, then taking the piss out of the local league cricketers, both allies and enemies, who took the game so seriously. Marsie had a competitive edge that would see him stare down lads in their twenties who were trying to knock him over with a cricket ball, and just giggle at them. Their sledging he'd encourage. Then he'd just shake his head and play shots into gaps in order to nick runs that any 'proper batsman' with any ambition to get the upper hand on his opponent would never dream of playing. He was there to win, by cunning and know-how more than physical strength.

Marsie was a little man. He stood no more than 5 foot 4, which meant that I towered over a foot above him. He'd grown up in racing and kept telling me of his early days, which he'd spent as a stable lad and eventually a jockey to Peter Cundell in the neighbouring village of Compton. His knowledge of racing, particularly his hush-hush contacts over in Ireland, meant that he was forever tipping me outsiders running at Listowel and Bellewstown. 'Bollocks!' was invariably my response to Marsie's latest tip, but he was invariably right. I'll never bet through hearing gossip, but Marsie always did well out of it. He kept all of his betting records scribbled down in a William Hill racing diary, the sort that fit so easily into a pocket. He kept everything in there. When I say everything in that diary, I mean *everything*. Cricket, racing, golf matches and stuff that Kerrie, his wife, required him to do. Marsie had his entire life mapped out in that diary.

I'd insisted upon christening him 'the Coffin Dodger' very early on in our relationship. He was the old lag in the cricket

Marsie – a bad loser in the face of a gracious winner

side and one of the most effective we had, in spite of his less than flamboyant batting technique. He always scored runs despite never hitting a ball with any eye-catching vigour, and he never let anyone down. That was quite annoying, as I and several other more physically strong teammates would attempt to smash the ball everywhere. Marsie played the percentages and he seldom got out to a silly, ambitious shot because he just wasn't as silly or ambitious as his far younger peers at West Ilsley Cricket Club.

If he was once young, dumb and wayward in his judgement I'd love to hear of it. He didn't entertain folly and he didn't drink. Coca-Cola was his tipple, although that might have explained the state of his teeth. 'Teeth like a row of bombed houses!' I'd shout from the pavilion when he'd played another match-winning innings. I didn't ever want him to know that I respected him greatly when he'd pulled us out of the shit again. Marsie's teeth were ready for the crematorium decades before he was.

Royal Windsor Racecourse stages meetings every Monday evening throughout the summer, meaning that I could do the horses with Mick in the morning and squeeze in a round of golf with Marsie at midday before a quick shower and an hour's drive to the racing. As I alluded to, I did eventually beat him 7–5 in our fifth summer of regular duels at Newbury & Crookham, but my agonising journey towards that victory cannot be imagined, having lost the previous four years on the bounce. He was both unbearable to be beaten by and unbearable to win against, although I'm probably much the same. It was the mind games that killed me, not the activity – I was a more talented cricketer and golfer than Marsie could ever be at his time in life, but he just got inside my head and made me crumble on all too many occasions. The banter was incessant. I had the ability to demolish him on the golf course. When I got it right, I'd be 150 yards ahead of him off the tee. I could reach the par fives in two shots if I had my game together, while he just bonked it straight, straight, straight down the middle, time after time after time. The monotonous bastard. If I played well, he merely stated that youth and leverage had been his undoing, and it was all down to the age gap. If he won, it was all down to my over-ambitious ego-driven attitude and his canny tactical nous. On Marsie's day, intelligence and know-how was the victor, with me cast in the role of the all-brawn, no-brained idiot.

Consequently, golf on Mondays dominated my thoughts once I started working for the yard. I relished Mondays back then. Not many people can say that. I'd had to abandon my laughs on the cricket field once I started working with my old man and began travelling to race meetings every Saturday but, with a wet sail and clear roads, I would often be able to get back to the club pavilion to rake over the ashes of our latest capitulation against another local village team and take the piss out of the boys, and Marsie in particular.

Marsie seldom failed, but I'd rattle down the motorways after racing with hope in my heart that he'd had a stinker that afternoon with either bat or ball – hopefully both. His teammates could always be relied upon to fill me in if Marsie had made any sort of an error. People loved taking the piss out of him because he was so good at taking the piss out of them. It was their chance of a little payback. Marsie's occasional failures brought me so much joy and occasionally, hopefully, they would still be distracting him when we teed off at midday the following Monday.

I vividly remember driving back from Doncaster on a gloriously sunny Saturday and parking the car right outside the pavilion, only to enter the clubhouse and be told that Marsie had been rushed to hospital. Apparently he'd been struck on the head by a short-pitched delivery from a rather useful local lad who had cricketing ability and age on his side – Marsie's least popular type of opponent.

I found this news rather amusing – until he still hadn't returned for over an hour and his bag in the dressing room remained as he'd left it. Alan Bloor, another local stalwart of the village, had driven Marsie to the hospital and he recalls with relish the moment they returned. Marsie saw my car in front of the pavilion. 'Oh bollocks! Fucking Channon's here,' he said, mortified in the passenger seat.

When he walked, or more accurately shuffled in, I was watching the telly in the corner, unaware of him until the laughter erupted. What I witnessed as I turned round was the most joyous sight I'd ever laid my eyes on. He was standing there with a bandage on his head and a look of complete defeat on his face. I can't remember speaking. I laughed louder than I ever had before. When I eventually gathered some sort of composure, he just said, deadpan, 'Don't tell Kerrie.'

Magic for me, misery for Marsie

Fucking hell I laughed. Total joy and total misery only a foot apart. That was a moment containing all of life's magic. Someone even took a photo of it.

The photo encapsulates the fun he brought to my life. It was the moment when Marsie knew he looked so ridiculous that he had no defence against my vicious bullying. In that moment I was Benny Hill slapping the bald bloke. That photo is the screen-saver on my phone to this day. It was probably the last day of summer we had together in that sort of rare form, because Marsie and I didn't do winters. If playing either golf or cricket required a pullover or standing about because of a rain delay, Marsie knew I wouldn't be interested. Therefore, between the months of October and the start of May, we'd rarely speak and never saw each other. It wasn't like that. We were good friends but we never socialised and never visited each other's houses. Our age gap certainly didn't demand it.

Just before the Flat season began, at the start of March 2014, I got a text from him:

I don't think the Coffin Dodger can dodge this one.

Now, he'd send the odd text about our runners or the way they'd been ridden from time to time, but he'd never send something so random or spine-chilling as that. I sent a text back:

What?

I'm in Royal Berks. Doesn't look good.

That rattled me. I phoned him immediately. I was with the two-year-olds who were trotting round the indoor school at West Ilsley at the time. It was a Tuesday.

'Hello,' he answered.

'Marsie, what the fuck is going on?'

'I'm in the hospital. Not great.'

'What is it?'

'Bile duct, hopefully; cancer for sure. I'm in trouble.'

'I'm on my way.'

Obviously I was late, I usually am, and it used to drive Marsie mad. I found him in his pyjamas drinking a can of Coke on the end bed of his ward. 'That'll rot your teeth,' I said.

'Fuck off,' he giggled.

He told me that he'd 'clogged up' a bit in the New Year and things hadn't improved and that, within the space of a fortnight, Kerrie had begun to urge him to sort himself out. It took more than one trip to the doctor's to convince them that something was seriously wrong, until he had what sounded like a spasm fit and was rushed in to Reading. The long and the short of it was he had cancer – probably in the bile duct, but if it wasn't, the pancreas. That would mean curtains, but he would know more in a week or so.

Our friendship wasn't so funny any more. I remember being very selfish and thinking that I was too young to have this happen to a friend. I went to see him on the Thursday week when he finally got back to his home in Thatcham. He showed me aroun the lovely garden and told me that his pension plan and li insurance would see Kerrie all right if he wasn't there any mo Kerrie was far, far younger than Marsie and was still out at w when he was telling me all of this. I was bemused because the bugger looked like he could play golf that afternoon.

'Basically, the bile duct is right next to the pancreas. I've growth in the bile duct and if they don't get rid of it, it'll to the pancreas, and that will be the end of it. That said, can get to it, I'll have at least another ten years. The wo scenario is that I'll die on the table. Or, I could do noth a bit of chemo and waste away in a couple of years. I backed a horse each way, so if Kerrie agrees, I'm g for it.'

We watched the racing in his front room that after Twiston-Davies's ride, finishing second on Lincoln, scrutiny at Wolverhampton. 'He rides well, but h opinion until he gets experience,' was Marsie's ver

And then he spoke to me about me. He'd n before. It was bang on the button and made me understated yet intelligent man he was. He assess my weaknesses and my future. He also explaine ways to cope with insecurity. He said some o but I'll keep that to myself. It's very personal.

He nailed my life to the floor that afternoon.

Then Kerrie came home. I called Marsie 'John' in front of her (which was bizarre) and that was the end of our friendship, until after Monday's operation. He went to hug me at the door as I left and, obviously, I told him to fuck off – he had many more coffins to dodge as far as I was concerned. I shook his hand, declined his offer of the 200 Benson & Hedges he'd decided he wouldn't ever smoke, and I exchanged numbers with Kerrie, who would call me after the operation.

April Fool's Day in 2014 was a work morning and first lot were walking home down the sand track on Hodcott Down. It was far too early for good news, about half-seven. Kerrie's number rang:

'Hi, Kerrie.'

'Hi, Mick.'

'How is he?'

'Um, well, um, John died this morning. He got through the operation, but his blood pressure dropped and that was it. I'm so sorry, but he'd have wanted you to know.'

John Marston loved his wife. I'll never forget our final conversation. I should have bought the 200 B&H he offered me.

At the West Ilsley Christmas Gentlemen's Lunch of 2014 I was appointed 'poet laureate', which meant that I had to come up with a ditty to entertain the Harrow regulars over the cheese, port and brandy. I decided to do a review of 2014 and ended with this as my closing prose:

And we'll all talk of Marsie, the 'Coffin Dodger' himself, such a fit sporting man, not known for poor health.

We played cricket and golf and laughed quite a lot, taking the piss every time one flayed a stray shot.

He was funny but brutal, his mind games unique, taking every advantage under that cap with its peak.

A wry smile one moment, abuse then came next, how I'll never forget receiving that text.

'I'm in Royal Berks today and I've been here a week, a rare shot to nothing, the surgeons do seek.'

We watched the racing together in Thatcham that day, his fate it was sealed but we knew not of which way.

And as things transpired Marsie wouldn't pull through but words can't describe what he left me and you.

That grin and that frame, a short man in long trousers, a laugh that showed teeth, like a row of bombed houses.

He was cute, brave and busy – a diminutive mentor, Old Marsie, that dwarf batting out in the centre.

After the funeral, I was gobsmacked. Marsie had always prattled on about how he beat the legendary Australian jockey Scobie Breasley in a match race at Sandown Park when he was a kid: the great Scobie Breasley riding an odds-on shot only to be beaten by a 16-year-old called John Marston – yeah, right. 'Bollocks with your Scobie Breasley bullshit!' was my usual response when he was playing his regular mind games on that tricky approach shot to the dog-leg eighth hole at Newbury & Crookham.

At Marsie's wake in The Swan there was an old newspaper photo pinned next to the bar amidst a collage of photos showing Marsie through the ages. It was a crinkled, stained clipping that showed Scobie Breasley aboard a horse called Ocean Diamond. He was trailing in the wake of an outsider called Early Bid, who the caption described as having run out a 'comfortable winner'.

The jockey on Early Bid was identified as 'J. Marston'.

What a lad indeed.

MORPHINE

GREAT WESTERN HOSPITAL, SWINDON, MONDAY
31 AUGUST 2015

A wet and windy Monday at Epsom, a winner in the form of Mick's own Potternello, ridden by Silvestre de Sousa, and a conversation with jockey John Egan that amazed me. Well, I suppose it didn't, really, but at times I'm unsure as to whether I'm living on a different planet. The last week has been all about doing the horses in the morning, driving to the races in the afternoon and then visiting the old man in Swindon.

Things haven't been easy for him but, on the whole, the operation was a success. The surgeon had to take out far more than he'd anticipated. The carcinoid had also spread to his appendix, so that was removed along with a twelve-inch section of his intestines. I'm told that although many class it as a cancer, it is very slow-growing and incredibly rare. That should be the end of the matter as well, with a bit of luck. At least that's what my optimistic side is telling me. It's now just getting the old man to accept his fate for the next two or three months – that is going to be the hard part. Can he rest up for that long? I'm very doubtful, and the visits I've made so far haven't offered much hope.

There was a commotion in one of the hospital rooms as I entered the Shalbourne Suite on Thursday. As I made my way down to room seven at the end of the corridor I passed a few scurrying nurses who were clearly dealing with something of an urgent medical nature in room three. Then, as I carried on walking and that commotion died down, another one arose as I approached the open door of room seven.

'I'm sorry, but this isn't good enough!' The old man was sitting up in bed and clearly administering a bollocking to a nurse who had obviously heard it all before. There was blood on the sheets beside him, clearly from his wrist where the cannula had leaked and the drip had been dislodged. 'I've been like this for over half an hour and it's not fucking good enough. I've had visitors in and they've seen me like this and it's not fucking good enough.' His voice was slurred and he was as high as a kite. I had to intervene: 'Mick, calm down. It's only a bit of blood. They're a bit busy further along the corridor and you're getting yourself in a state.'

'But I've been sitting here like this for fucking ages.' This was like a toddler's tantrum in Tesco. A patient voice intervened. I couldn't be a nurse. 'I'm very sorry but we've just had a bit of an emergency down the hall. I'll get this cleaned up and everything will be sorted in no time.'

Mick jumped in again: 'But it shouldn't fucking happen. Look at me! There's blood everywhere.' He was clearly off his tits.

I'd just about had enough by now and I'd only been there for thirty seconds: 'Mick, listen to me. You're on morphine, it's not as bad as you think, and we can get this sorted. Now let her do her job.'

He started to back down. 'I'm sorry. This is my son, Jack. He'd handle things a bit better than me. I know it's not your fault, love. I'm very sorry. Thank you.'

She changed the sheets in no time, all the while in relative silence – the sort of sulky silence when embarrassment dawns at the back end of an outburst.

'Thank you, love, thank you very much. Appreciate it, thank you.'

She left the room. He was sitting there, like he had been since Wednesday, tired and pale, a plastic jug of water and a cup for company. He looked dreadful.

'You all right, then?'

'Yeah! But I was like that for ages!' His rage rose again: 'Peter and Patrick were in to see me and I looked a right state. It's not fucking good enough!'

I had to stamp it out: 'That's sorted now though, isn't it? Apart from that, is everything all right?'

'Telly's crap.'

'Is the telly not working?'

'It works, but they haven't got *At The Races*.'

Typical Mick.

Things are going well enough in his absence at work, and we're having winners. Because Mick is out of it for long parts of the day, I've overseen exercise in the mornings, done entries and declarations and rung around to speak to the jockeys every day ahead of their rides in the afternoon. Not that I ought to have bothered with the jockeys, though. John Egan won on Persun at Newmarket on Friday evening and he came up to me in the winners' enclosure after Potternello's success at Epsom this afternoon: 'How's your dad? Is he *all right*?' He said this with a very concerned look on his face. I immediately adopted the sort of body language that would belie any sign of weakness: 'Yeah! He's fine!' I don't think I'd entirely put his mind at ease. 'Why?'

'Well, I spoke to him on the phone on Friday and he didn't sound too good.'

'He *rang* you?'

'Well, I phoned him and left a message, then I spoke to you and he phoned straight after.'

'Right.' I was a bit pissed off. 'What did he say?'

'I'm not too sure. Is he OK? His voice was kind of slurred and he didn't make a lot of sense.'

'Yeah, well, he's just not too well at the moment, a bit rough. It's nothing too serious.'

'Well, just tell him the filly did it real nice and she'll win again.'

'Will do. Thanks, John.'

He walked off and it was clear that he knew something serious had gone on. I was trying to think clearly about what on earth the old man was thinking, but it quickly became clear when I arrived that evening that he wasn't thinking too much. I had to broach the subject. 'Why the fuck are you talking to jockeys?'

'What?'

'I said, why the fuck are you talking to jockeys? You sound like you're pissed at the moment. It's hardly helping us to sweep this under the carpet.'

'I haven't spoken to any jockeys!'

'You spoke to John Egan on Friday!'

'I never.'

'You did!'

'I never.'

'You did! He spoke to me today and was concerned about you.'

'I might have talked to him, but I've got to keep things normal. The sales are coming up and I don't want anyone to think I'm not well.'

I took in the scene in front of me. My old man in a hospital gown, connected to a drip, wires everywhere, oxygen tubes up his nose, and his bruised and battered arthritic feet sticking out at the bottom of his hospital bed. How could anyone possibly think he wasn't well?

'You're on morphine, Mick. That *isn't* normal. John Egan spoke to me and asked because you sound pissed and incoherent.'

'I'm not on morphine! I've not been on it for days.' A loud noise sounded: 'Beeeep!' He'd pressed the trigger to administer morphine from the machine behind him. This was both stressful and impossible.

'LAWRIE'S JUST CALLED'

THURSDAY 1 JUNE 1995

I was playing Scrabble with Nicky in Mick and Jill's kitchen at Saxon Gate Stables in Upper Lambourn. I became quite an adept Scrabble player that summer, along with reading books and finally mastering Donkey Kong on the Nintendo. This was mainly because I had an awful lot of time on my hands after being discharged from the Bristol Royal Infirmary. There wasn't that much for me to do apart from play Scrabble, read books and play computer games because the halo brace that I'd had drilled into my skull less than a month before meant that I didn't really feel like going out in public very often. This was a contraption that meant I couldn't wash my hair for three months. Mick began calling me 'Herman Munster'. He was right as well. I felt like a freak. I'd get odd looks from people just walking across the car park as I headed into the BRI for outpatient appointments, so going home to live with Mum in Southampton wasn't really an option for the time being. Mick's house at Saxon Gate overlooked the adjoining stables and provided the privacy in which I could hide myself away and wait for everything to blow over. I was very self-conscious, not only because I was carrying a metal contraption around on my head but also because some of the publicity that my stupidity and injuries had attracted underlined what a total idiot I'd been.

'All right, son! You're famous then!' Mick Quinn was on the phone taking the piss mercilessly with a blend of concern and immense relish. 'A mate of mine said you made the '*Currant Bun*' the other day!' He was calling from Greece, where he was signing for a team called PAOK Thessaloniki. He was nearing the end of his football career but clearly wanted the low down on what had *actually* happened. It was true, as well: I was tabloid fodder, with page seven of the *Sun* screaming 'MICK CHANNON'S KID BUSTS HIS NECK SLEEPWALKING'. The family were so proud of me. 'So come on, then. What were you up to? Were you trying to get out of a bird's bedroom, or, more worryingly, were you trying to climb into one?' Typical Quinny.

I could understand the fascination. We'd been contacted by loads of newspapers, with the *News of the World* even offering a free holiday for Anna and me if I opened up and told them the 'true story' of what had actually happened. Anna took the calls. 'Exactly how many times *has* Michael tried LSD?' was a typical line of questioning. We never went on that holiday.

It was about lunchtime and Mick came downstairs having showered after the morning's exercise with the horses. He was wearing a pair of baggy jogging bottoms and a T-shirt. He was red-faced, clearly very emotional. Our game of Scrabble ceased almost immediately. 'Lawrie's just called.' He was holding back tears and coughing for no apparent reason whatsoever. One phone call from Dad's old Southampton manager shouldn't have had this sort of an impact, but it was clear that something was terribly wrong. I'm only guessing here but Mick was probably trying to hold back any signs of weakness from his two children. He was failing quite spectacularly.

'Bobby's died.'

I don't remember any explanation or what he said next. I do remember him spending a lot of time upstairs on his own. I just remember the Scrabble board, the kitchen and my sister.

'What?' Bobby was a mainstay of our childhood. Nicky and I had known Bobby and Jan Stokes for ever. Jan was Mum's best friend and Bobby was Mick's. Bobby was always my hero, always my friend and always around. He was one of the first people I remember as a small boy. I learnt the word 'sausages' from Bobby and Jan. I developed a deep love of sausages and Bobby would always remind me of his role in that: it was our own private joke that he'd always bring up when he came round to our house, when we were drunk at my eighteenth birthday party, when I became his driver, when we went to Wembley.

By scoring the winner for Southampton at Wembley in 1976, Bobby became a part of folklore. He'd be invited to charity events and people would come up to him and thank him for giving them the best day of their lives. Bob would just smile and sign autographs while I'd stand by his side drinking a glass of Coke with the keys to my Fiesta 1.3 Ghia in my pocket.

Peter Osgood had appointed me as Bob's driver. Ossie had clearly tired of driving down the M27 to pick Bobby up at his home in Portsmouth for all the social functions they'd attend together, and once I'd passed my driving test I was more than happy to fulfil the role. That's one of the strange things about Bob – he remained in Pompey all of his life, in spite of the fact that he'd scored the winner for Southampton.

Bobby never learnt to drive, even though he'd been given a car for scoring the winner in the Cup final, and he never changed, which only makes him greater in my eyes. He was so ordinary in the most extraordinary way, simply because he remained totally normal. His only trouble was, he wanted to be a footballer for ever, because that was what he was good at – it was what made him happy.

He'd split up with Jan by the time I started driving him, and he'd not helped himself, to be honest. His drinking had escalated although only Jan knew of its true toll. The fact that his death still stirs sadness within me to this day underlines how his departure, while inevitable now we all have hindsight, didn't seem quite so real at the time.

Bob was just Bob. Always smiling, always kind, always so lovable. What he couldn't do, however, was find something to replace football once his playing days were behind him. It takes a lot for any sportsman to become a person in the real world after the cheers subside. Bobby just fell short.

For a couple of years I'd drive him everywhere, and my abiding memory is of picking him up on the Sunday immediately before my A level exams. Ossie called me and said that we had to meet at Wembley by ten o'clock, and that he and Bally would meet us there – my A levels were important, but nothing was more important than a day at Wembley with Bob. Plus, Ossie didn't really give me much of an option. It was more of an order, not an invitation.

The massive wooden gates at Wembley were open that morning, unlike the day when Norwich had met Sunderland seven years previously. It was a mild early summer morning and we were there to coach inner-city youngsters from north London ahead of a charity match later in the day. The place was deserted but for a hundred-odd kids, a real ethnic mix of London schoolchildren, all gathered together in the centre circle of the pitch as they were introduced to the four coaches, whom they knew nothing about, by their local schoolteacher: Alan Ball (FA Cup runner-up in 1968 and 1972), Peter Osgood (FA Cup winner in 1970 and

1976), Graham Paddon (FA Cup winner, 1975) and Bobby Stokes (FA Cup match-winner, 1976). The kids just looked at them nonplussed. The coaching session lasted for almost two hours. I remember that Bally and Graham, being midfielders, set up their coaching sessions based on possession and keep-ball in the middle of the pitch, while Ossie took the goal at the far end because Bobby insisted on coaching his session by the goal at the tunnel end where he'd scored his winner 16 years and one month previously. He was so funny that day.

I was his 'runner'. I laid out the cones and fetched the balls and did all of his demonstrations for him. Bob just didn't want the limelight – all he really wanted to achieve was a sense of fun among the 30 kids gathered on the edge of the penalty box. Basically, all he did was get them to score as many times as possible at Wembley. He had no interest in improving them as footballers; he just wanted them to have fun, full stop.

That would have been fine but for Bally's high-pitched voice echoing around the old stadium demanding excellence throughout, while Bob spent most of the morning laughing and making me out to be a bully for stopping shots that he didn't want me to save. Bobby's coaching position remained the same throughout as each of the four groups interchanged between the four coaches. I can still see Bobby standing just outside of the penalty box berating any of the kids who missed the target: 'How can you miss from there? I beat Alex Stepney from *here*! And it was with my left foot!'

Not one of the kids had a clue who he was. I laughed all morning.

Once the coaching session was over we had lunch, then loads of former players arrived as a small crowd gathered for the charity match. We all got changed in a room adjacent to the bar behind the royal box, so I never actually got to get changed in the dressing rooms at Wembley.

I didn't mention that I played at Wembley did I?

I played at Wembley.

The Old Wembley. The good one. The one where my dad played for England. The one where Bobby scored the Cup winner for Saints.

They named the team and Bally, Graham and Bobby were all in the starting eleven. Ossie couldn't play because his knees were knackered, but he was philosophical about the disappointment because he'd had a rather enjoyable lunch. So had Bobby, now I mention it. He sidled up to me. I was sitting there, next to my pair of adidas World Cup boots. Bob said, 'Here, I've failed a fitness test today so I'm going to be Ossie's assistant manager. I want you to go out and play for me.' He was grinning like only Bobby could, the deepest of smile lines beneath his typically foppish fringe – a smile that never seemed to age him.

'Really?'

'Yeah. I've had my day here, now you go out and play.'

I played centre-half and marked Micky Hazard (FA Cup winner 1982) while being bollocked by Graham and Bally for giving the ball away too often. My abiding memory, though, is of Bobby giving me the thumbs-up from the bench every time I won a header or just got stuck in. I was playing on my nerves, if the truth be told.

Bobby was drinking a can of lager.

I feel so sad that he died so young, only 44.

Bobby's smile is still with me.

A new stable block was being built at our stud farm outside Southampton – I guess it would be about 1983. Mick had just started playing for Norwich, Uncle Phil was there and Dad's two

Bobby, Brian and Mick – teammates, dog owners and stable builders

best friends, Bobby and Brian O'Neil, were roped in to help. It was a self-assembling timber construction and I remember Brian setting the concrete base and there being loads of bickering for several weekends until they finally got to the stage where the felt roof needed to be tacked on. This was where the worlds of football and amateur stable construction came together.

Brian O'Neil was a scrapper, a top footballer but he has always prided himself on battling away and picking the fights others couldn't win. Back then as a player, and still to this day, Brian O'Neil remains very protective of my old man. Bobby was the runner – he'd work all day long for his friends – a totally selfless individual. Phil was like me, not quite good enough to be a footballer. I'm proud to say that I'm like my uncle Phil. And then there was Mick. Standing there, telling everyone else what to do.

It was a Sunday morning. Brian was holding the ladder and Bobby was on the roof being told by Mick how to nail the felt to the plywood roof. Phil, meanwhile, was taking the piss out of him. I was laughing. I was eight or nine.

'Stop fucking about, Stokesy!' Mick was getting agitated. The stables had taken nearly a month to complete by then, and there was Bob moaning, a fag hanging out of the corner of his mouth trying to nail some felt into boards of plywood.

'Why am I always up the ladder?' he moaned.

'Get the thing done and we can fuck off to the Fox for a pint!' was the old man's response.

That felt roof got done in double-quick time.

They are three friends I'll always remember as a kid – Brian, Bobby and Mick. One tough, one toiler and one talented. All quite mad in their own unique ways.

I didn't go to Bobby's funeral because I had a load of metal screws in my skull. In many ways it helped. Because I wasn't there I didn't get any true sense of closure, which I'm glad about. I just think he's still in Portsmouth. I think of him every time I head to the races at Goodwood or Fontwell. I'm usually in a hurry, but some day I'll pop in and see him and have a cup of tea.

I'll always remember dropping Bob off at his parents' house in Paulsgrove after a charity cricket match. If you drive past Pompey from Southampton on the M27, Paulsgrove is perched high up on the chalk slopes of the housing estate on your left. I've only been there once. It takes a while to turn off the M27 and drive up that hill.

'I'll bet you weren't popular coming back here after the Cup final!' I said, as he was getting out of the Fiesta.

'To be honest, it was the best moment of my life.'

I thought he was joking. 'Really?'

'Yeah. My mum and dad were here, all the neighbours. They were so proud of me. They put on a street party right here.' He was pointing at the open gardens between the backed terraced houses, all nicely lined by lawns and rose bushes.

'Really?'

'Yeah!'

I couldn't believe it. It was lovely to see him so nostalgic. No hint of bitterness.

My mind's eye sees Bobby still standing between those terraced houses remembering the time when he was on top of the world. An ordinary hero. Not many of us have been there.

June 1995 wasn't all tragedy, though. Grandad Jack came through on his promise of taking me to the Malt Shovel, just over the road from Saxon Gate, to get 'thoroughly pissed'. Trouble was, I wasn't the one who got pissed. Jack was never really a drinker although he loved a pint of Salisbury's. He'd chat to anyone would Jack, and people genuinely enjoyed his company. He was an old-school country lad, nothing like his sons, Mick and Phil. The pair of them might be morphing into their dad as age envelops them both physically and follically, but I think the post-war generation which they represent has plenty to do with a far more outward perspective on the world around them than Jack ever had.

I'd just come off antibiotics – six weeks was more than enough – and the day arrived when my grandad rose from the sofa, buttoned up his green cardigan and signalled that the time had come: 'Come on, then. Let's go over the Malt and have those beers.' He'd clearly been looking forward to this drinking session.

There were a few stable lads having a pint in the Malt Shovel after morning exercise, but it was quiet enough as Jack put his hand in his pocket and pulled out a tenner. That was his idea of a major session – ten pounds. He wasn't far wide of the mark, though, as he proceeded to get rather drunk rather quickly. After

Grandad Jack

three pints of Salisbury's, Clive the landlord suggested that he went back to the house for a lie down. Jack was no trouble, he was just pissed. There's a small step at the door of the Malt Shovel that leads out onto the road, with a pasture field opposite. As with many country lanes there is a drainage ditch along the far side of the road, and I remember walking out into bright summer sunshine and waiting for Jack to finish his goodbyes. I was just standing there looking out into the paddock.

'Oh bugger!' was all I heard behind me, but I couldn't look round because my head was in traction. The next thing I knew, the staggering figure of my grandad proceeded to wobble straight past me, across the road and straight into the ditch, just his arse and legs sticking out of the gully, which was overgrown with nettles.

It's difficult to pull your 78-year-old grandad out of a ditch with a halo brace screwed into your skull. Thankfully Clive offered me some assistance, and I supported Grandad the 100 yards or so over to Mick's house.

'That bloody step!' complained Jack.

'That bloody Salisbury's, you mean!'

'Just don't tell Grandma.'

I remember thinking that would be hard to avoid due to the state he was in – the nettle stings beginning to visibly flare up all over his bald head. He was a funny man, even if he didn't always know it.

RECLAIMING CONTROL

THURSDAY 17 SEPTEMBER 2015

The 'couple or three days' that Mick said he'd be in the hospital following the operation dragged on to almost a week before he was allowed to come home. He was told to have three weeks off, entire rest. He managed three days.

We've done OK in his absence. The good form of the horses has continued, with Potternello, Persun and our owner Garry Brandt enjoying a double with Harlequin Striker winning at Epsom and Harlequeen winning at Goodwood. Garry, his wife Susanne and his mum were with me at Goodwood and I'll not forget Garry jumping on me as Harlequeen won easily by five lengths on her racecourse debut. Moments like that – the joy people get from racing – make it all worthwhile.

The downside is the disappointments, and Malabar's trip to New York for the Grade 2 Sands Point Stakes proved pointless and pathetic. I could say far more here but I won't. It's not something I'd want published and not something worth saying. A bitter disappointment that will take a long time to get over.

On a brighter note, Zuzinia, Masterson and Willsy also won during this period as the old man insisted on coming into the office for as long as he could before shuffling off home to rest. Which was daft, really, because he soon managed to get an infection that has set his recovery back by weeks. Perhaps the medical staff were right in telling him to have complete rest. Obviously he knew better. His arthritis has flared up as well, so he's had a very rough time of things, but he can't stay away. The horses are fit by now and the disappointment of the early season results now favours our horses. They've all come down to handicap marks that they can win off. They don't need training, they just need placing in the right races. Even I'm capable of that.

That's helped Silvestre de Sousa as well. He's been terrific this season and is miles out in front of the race for the jockeys' championship, winning on plenty of our horses in the process. He's been a great help. A tiny man but a big personality, I get the impression that he thinks he can win on anything at the moment, and the horses have certainly responded. All he wants to know is what each horse is like and how he can get the best out of them. Sometimes he's not even wanted to know that. In the weighing room at Epsom, before he rode Potternello, I collected the saddle from him and asked, 'What are you going to do on this filly?' to which he just smiled and said, 'Win.' That was good enough for me.

Charlie Bishop, too, is profiting from the form of the horses, and his confidence along with that of Danny Cremin has soared in recent weeks. The whole staff – although kept in the dark these last few weeks, and visibly shocked at the state of the boss when they've seen him in the office – have been terrific. They've made life very easy.

Today wasn't exactly easy, though, because some of the old Mick has returned to regain a bit of control. He was in a foul mood all morning and insisted on coming up the gallops for the first time since the operation. He criticised everything. That horse shouldn't join that one, this filly shouldn't lead, he can't ride that horse, he's useless, that one is doing too much, that colt isn't doing enough . . . on and on and on.

I can honestly say that I've done my best. It doesn't feel that way, though.

We had a loose horse during second lot and I set after it as it galloped towards the road. I hit a couple of major ridges at about 40 miles an hour and eventually caught it by the gate after some bone-crunching impacts at the bottom of the gallop. I walked it home but the old man, who was sitting alongside me in the wagon during the pursuit, was badly shaken up in his fragile state. To be honest, and I hate myself for feeling this way, I couldn't give a shit. I feel for him, and I know he's been through a dreadful ordeal, but he does this all the time: creating conflict, searching for enemies, seeking out subjects to blame. In many ways it's a positive sign in terms of Mick's physical recovery, but it's dented my optimism that he might have found any sort of perspective on life in general.

'THAT FUCKER'LL WIN THE DERBY'

SUNDAY 11 OCTOBER 2015

We've heard the same story on countless occasions.

'Fucking good horse that! I'm telling you, that fucker'll win the Derby!'

Mick still owns and breeds a few horses. He obviously trains them as well.

Now, from his perspective, he's never bred a bad one, and has been cruelly denied Classic glory through myriad reasons and a long line of culprits. Jockeys mainly. It's all their fault: 'You've gotta give the fucker a chance! Not ride it like a dickhead!'

There's a long list of horses on this roster of broken dreams: Narborough, Fraamington, Arantes, Nutbush, Rated, Lucky Leigh, Green Army. Some were decent, some were awful and we still have that sort of range of quality at the yard today: from Harrison down to Walrus Gumboot.

Now, for all bar Mick, the general consensus is that Walrus Gumboot is one of the slowest and least enthusiastic horses to ever look through a bridle. He's about to turn four in the new year, he's never seen a racecourse and certainly isn't a great fan of daily exercise on the gallops. In his two years at West Ilsley, he's basically concentrated on eating and having time off. Not a bad life, all considered, but hardly the one we'd like him to live.

He's big, burly and cumbersome, not an athlete at all, but Mick is adamant there's a racehorse there.

For all of his shouting, screaming, unpleasantness and all round stubborn behaviour, this is by far his worst trait. He trains *every single horse*. What's more, he will persevere with *every single horse* until it wins a race.

It's a well-rehearsed list of quotes that I hear time and again:

'There's a race for every horse.'

'They all deserve a chance.'

'He's not shown much at home, but a race will sharpen him up.'

'You wait, when he learns to settle, he'll be all right.'

'The ground was all against him. When we get a bit of rain, it'll be different.'

'I might try him on the all-weather.'

'The penny's not dropped with him yet.'

'You wait for next year, he'll be all right.'

'Have we got the trip wrong?'

'Stall twelve! He's got no chance with that draw!'

'Have you seen the handicap mark? He's given him sixty-two! What fucking chance has he got? Get me the fucking handicapper on the phone!'

This attitude, as wonderfully optimistic as it is, doesn't help.

There is plenty of emphasis placed on strike rates among trainers, and while a 20 per cent strike rate of winners will always be out of reach for a yard training horses of our calibre, we tend to flirt with single figures, primarily because Mick tries so hard with *incredibly* moderate horses.

I liked Imperial Spirit. He was very moderate but was kind, willing and sound. Mick didn't breed him, but he's good friends with the guy who did, John Coggan, and set his heart on winning a race with this little horse. *For two whole years.*

For the last six months, he didn't even charge the syndicate, who had long given up on their horse winning back some of their training fees. That's how stubborn Mick can be. In the meantime, our strike rate became worse and worse as Imperial Spirit was entered in the worst races on this planet and still came up short.

Until 21 September 2013. What a night at Wolverhampton that was. On his twenty-sixth start, Imperial Spirit made all to beat ten opponents (none of whom had ever won a race between them) in one of the worst handicaps in the history of horserac-ing. The scenes in the office were remarkable, as Mick celebrated like he'd won the lottery and proceeded to remind everyone who had long lost interest in his quest for glory with Imperial Spirit, *'I fucking told you that little horse would win!'*

That might seem like a heart-warming tale of perseverance over pride, but the truth of the matter is it's a nightmare when trying to attract any new business. If you were to look at the raw statistics in any business, would you send a horse to a trainer with a 15 per cent strike rate or a trainer with a 9 per cent strike rate?

Exactly.

That's what I used to try to impress on the old man. He would occasionally teeter on the brink of agreeing that I might have a point, but he'd always pull himself back with the repost, 'Statis-tics are a load of bollocks! Michael Stoute wouldn't have won with Imperial Spirit!' And he'd be right. Sir Michael Stoute would have yard cats capable of winning more races than Impe-rial Spirit ever did, but he wouldn't train *them* either, yet Mick's view of how he campaigns his horses and, more importantly, the quality of horses that he perseveres with, is one that really doesn't help the business.

In fairness, he started with seven horses that only had thir-teen eyes between them. Three legs, one eye, he'd train any-

Harrison

thing. He'd been an owner and a breeder himself and built the training business up by working far harder than he ever did in his first career, and that mindset of hard graft and perseverance, once cemented, will never leave him. In terms of public perception though, he probably trains far too many low-grade horses to ever attract the eye of a fiercely ambitious new owner, because he loves winning with slow horses, and he never gives up on them. I suppose that's admirable, and today, at Goodwood, his latest 'champion' homebred won in fine style against a homebred belonging to Prince Khalid Abdullah. You can see where this is going, can't you?

By the stallion Sixties Icon, Harrison is a very good-looking two-year-old who is better than average on the gallops at home. I'd say he's 'nice'; Mick, however, has already predicted that he's going to win the Dante Stakes at York in May next year before heading to the Derby at Epsom in June. To be fair, he said he'd need his first run to get to grips with the job in hand last month at Salisbury, and he also said that he'd win today, so we're bang on course to become millionaires, because he told me this morning to tell the press when he won that, 'The fucker's not for sale.'

I didn't tell them exactly *that*, but I certainly laid it on thick in a television interview on Racing UK afterwards.

While I'm at it, that's another side of the game that we really can improve on. Mick's attitude to the press is dismissive at best, abysmal at its very worst. He simply has no time for them: 'They're all a waste of fucking time. You say something and they make it sound like you've said something else. They write bollocks and they certainly talk bollocks, so fuck 'em.'

I disagree. I'm not a great fan of being interviewed but I'm of the opinion that you might as well say something for them to take away. And he's right: an awful lot of it is 'bollocks'. I try to point out that the vast majority of new trainers talk plenty of bollocks, some of them don't even realise how much bollocks they are talking and some combine bullshit with bollocks. While some don't even realise that they are talking bollocks, some might genuinely believe that they hold the key to the racehorse in their hands, and that they're providing journalists with access to their infinite wisdom in a series of hallowed sound bites. Whatever bollocks they come up with, though, they get good press as a result – and they keep getting good press. What's wrong with that?

If you make the job easy, the press will work *for* you. I know that for a fact.

When I was a journalist at Granada, the very last places I wanted to go to were Manchester United or Liverpool. The press officers, the accreditation, the dismissive responses, the hostility towards the media, the lack of anything vaguely insightful all left me cold. No wonder that Mick seldom gets popular press. (Not that he gets negative press either.) I try to impress on him that I've been that journalist. Whenever I was asked to phone up Liverpool for an interview with Gérard Houllier, I was the one who turned round and said, 'Fuck off, get James or Mike to do it. I'm going to Rochdale, they might get in the play-offs.'

Places like Rochdale had very happy friendly people. Therefore, I'd do the lower league stories, where you get a cup of tea and a sit down with the manager in his office, and perhaps a funny interview with the groundsman or the tea lady. I'd even join in a training session, particularly when Andy Ritchie was manager at Oldham. They were proper stories – not a strangulated, five-minute confrontation over the forthcoming match against Villa and an update on the state of Patrik Berger's ongoing hamstring troubles. 'Start to wrap it up now, please,' would come the edict from the press officer after little or no topic of interest had been covered, so I'd come out with something bland and throw in, 'Message for the fans?' or 'What's the mood in the camp?' then go back, edit the six minutes into three minutes of vaguely interesting chat, stick some goals over the top and piss off home.

My point is, you don't get the press on your side unless you give them something to work with. If you provide them with anything half decent, even if it is 'bollocks', what harm can it do? Talking 'bollocks' is almost becoming essential.

I gave them plenty this afternoon. I made it light-hearted too, because I'd hate to be accused of talking bollocks – although I certainly was.

And what if the old man is right? What if Harrison does win the Derby next year? We'd be able to tarmac the main yard for a start – that would be great.

Mind you, he might be talking bollocks.

'WHAT'S WRONG WITH HIM?'

WEDNESDAY 14 OCTOBER 2015

Mick got back from the sales at Newmarket this afternoon. He left on Sunday and spent three days up there, buying seven horses in the Tattersalls Book 2 Sales. They cost, in total, just short of half a million quid. While that sounds ridiculous to the real world, it really isn't. It sounds like I'm pleading poverty, but we are way down the pecking order, and it's been a struggle, with Mick putting his neck on the line with half of them just to get horses into the yard to start afresh with new stock next year. We're already riding the homebred yearlings around the indoor school, a sure sign that although this season is yet to finish, the next one has already begun. It's bloody cold here in the winter.

More importantly, though, it was Mick's first venture out since the operation and, while he looks like a 66-year-old man who's had major surgery, at least he was there, moaning and grumbling as usual, complaining about the ridiculous price of horses. I'm glad he went, though, and it feels like a corner has been turned.

The only trouble is that when he returns after a few days away he wants to be updated on all of the horses. That's when things get frustrating. He's got such an active mind, with so many details (some important, some inconsequential) that once he's asked a question, he's already firing off another one, while also asking questions of others in the room at the same time. As a result, he takes nothing in.

He was sitting in the office during evening stables and started asking me about the horses.

'How's Scrutineer?'

'He's good, joined October Storm this morning.'

'Is he all right?'

'He's good.'

'What about Somersby?'

'He did two canters today.'

'Viva Steve?'

'He joined Knock House.'

'Knock House all right?'

'Fine.'

'Arnold Lane?'

'Fine.'

'Knight Of The Air?'

'Fine.'

'Fitzwilly?'

'Fine. They're all good.'

During all of this, he's looking through the sales horses and their prices and dealing with Gill over the finances. As a result, he's not listening to any of my replies, so I decided to nip it in the bud rather than go through every single one of the 80 horses left in training at this stage of the season.

'The only problem is Divine after her run at Newmarket. Nothing serious, just a bit stiff. She cantered this morning but I wasn't entirely happy. That's it, though – the rest of them are all perfect.'

'You're happy with them, then?'

'Apart from Divine, yes – all good.'

'How's Harrison?'

'Good.'

'Summer Icon?'

'Good.'

'Motdaw.'

'Good.'

'Exentricity?'

'Good.'

'Isabella Bird?'

'Good.'

'Sgt Reckless?'

'Good.'

He's still looking at the sales figures and scribbling away. Still throwing out random names of horses and not listening to my answers. 'How's Scrutineer?'

I'm now starting to lose the will to live. 'He's *fine*! You've already asked me about him!'

'About who?' Suddenly he starts to listen.

'Scrutineer!'

'What's wrong with Scrutineer?'

'NOTHING! The only problem out of the entire string is Divine.'

'What's wrong with her, then?'

'Nothing much – just a bit stiff after her run at Newmarket.'

'Oh. But you're happy with Scrutineer?'

'*Yes!*'

'Did he join today?'

And so it goes on. Doing my fucking head in.

That said, I'm genuinely chuffed to have him back. He's fiercely focused but incredibly vague all at the same time, which is an incredibly difficult skill to master. There must be some sort of a diagnosis for that.

THE BLAME GAME

MONDAY 19 OCTOBER 2015

We learn lessons in life through the mistakes we make. I certainly have anyway: don't text while drunk; don't sleep on a roof if you have a tendency to sleepwalk; don't set fire to your place of work; don't expect old men to change.

Today was a watershed in Mick's recovery. He drove the gallop wagon for the first time during morning exercise. He's bright, energetic and demoralisingly miserable again. His default demeanour is always so, particularly on a Monday morning. He's grumpy, aggressive and full of accusations. The search for an enemy is on today, real or imagined, to rage against, preferably to intimidate – at times like this he can be an incredibly unpleasant person to be around.

He had a driver to take him to the sales at Newmarket, but he's just driven himself off to Lavington Stud in Sussex, his first stint behind the wheel since the operation. He returned to the office before he left, swearing about his iPhone because he still can't work it, and once we got it going for him he sped off at his usual speed with it clamped to his ear.

I hate that phone. It was Jack and India's idea last Christmas. They thought their dad ought to upgrade the old brick he'd had for the last six years and that it was about time he joined the revolution. I hate that phone deeply. The alarm bells started ringing when I found him trying to activate it by swiping the back of it. This was a top of the range iPhone 6 with more apps and technology than he needed, so Jack gave him his old one because he claimed it would be a lot easier for him to use. I wish that hadn't happened, because that meant that Mick then had a phone with the same charger lead as I had. Inside three weeks he'd used and then lost no fewer than three charging leads and two wall plugs for his new phone and blamed everyone else for losing them. As a result, I was left with nothing to keep my own phone alive. It did my head in to such an extent that I had to get an upgrade so that I could have a phone with a different charger to him.

Mick's new (old) phone still doesn't work properly. I've suggested on numerous occasions that perhaps its owner is faulty, a possibility immediately dismissed amid a bluster of rage and frustration.

First lot this morning was far from a happy one. Three runners didn't win yesterday and they didn't win because they couldn't. They weren't good enough. The apprentices came in for plenty of abuse. Paddy Pilley rode a shocker (it was a shocker) but also got a bollocking, not only for that but for riding winners on other trainers' horses in recent weeks. Danny Cremin got a bollocking for his ride on Highlife Dancer that caused even me to intervene with reason.

'Highlife has never won off that handicap mark in his life, Mick.'

'Had a fucking great chance on that ground!'

'Not under that weight, he didn't.'

I'm talking reason, Mick changes tack: 'The kid's gone anyway. He's had a terrible attitude since he decided to leave.'

Indeed, Danny is moving on – to Australia at the end of this month. I'm pleased for him. His attitude hasn't been terrible either;

if anything, he's been great. Hope has long abandoned him and he seems to have accepted that. He's working away with the sort of freshness that only those newly freed of any ambition can, with a new, brighter future ahead of him. Mick no longer intimidates him either, and *that's* where his attitude has changed. He's had the big stick treatment for so long that bollockings no longer have any impact on him. He's stopped caring about his future with us, and I wish him well. He's a lovely lad, a fella with a great sense of humour. He'll be all right will Danny. He may not be a champion of the future but he'll earn a few quid riding horses for others.

I know why Mick has turned on him. It's the fact that he's leaving, he's no longer 'one of us', that he sees his life elsewhere, away from West Ilsley. It's as though Mick has been rejected and Danny is now a wolf in sheep's clothing. He's still with us, but already gone. Mick needs that.

You wouldn't believe it but the winners have continued to come as well. Viva Steve was our first winner over jumps on Saturday at Market Rasen, as the Flat season tails off and the National Hunt campaign begins to gain momentum. I needed Viva Steve to win, for myself more than anybody, even his owner Tim Radford. Knock House was beaten at odds-on at Fakenham on Friday and Mick was at his depressing best when the horse was beaten on his seasonal debut: 'The fucker blew up, he was short of work, plain and simple.'

I took that personally. It was as though I've not been doing my job correctly during Mick's recovery. As though not only have I not been doing my job properly but I'm not capable of it either. I'm the one with a bright outlook on most things. I'm the joker, the one with the bouncy demeanour, the clown.

But I'm not. I've worked my bollocks off. Granted, I've not been coming into the yard like a human hand grenade, and I've certainly done things in a different manner to the old man, but I know how to get a horse fit. Knock House was just beaten by a horse that had already had a run this year. That's not a crime and it's certainly not a sign that I'm incapable of preparing a horse. The difference since the operation is that I know I'm capable of it.

Not that I'm the next Henry Cecil, and nor does Monty Roberts call me for advice every morning, but I've been doing this for eight years, and if I didn't know the routine by now, I'd be seriously incompetent and certainly lacking in intelligence. That's why I took it personally. I took it personally because I no longer need Mick's assurances and approval. I don't need to hear praise or any credit for whatever it is that I do. I know I can do it. 'It's not rocket surgery or brain science,' as Mick once described it.

Two weeks ago, when he was only just starting to get better, Mick gave a scathing assessment of the condition of our jumpers: 'They're fat. Look at them, they're fucking fat. Fat horses don't win races.'

We worked them the next morning and when they were walking home he came out with, 'They're ready to go now, they look great.'

What a work morning that must have been: an incredible turn-around inside twenty-four hours, and just because *he* was there.

Since his operation we've had nineteen winners. That's not a bad ten weeks. I'm not even saying that I trained them either, but we've had a far better end to the season in view of the dismal start we all endured. The honest truth of the matter is that we'd have had those winners anyway. A shaved ape could have done what I have, with eight years of experience behind him. We have a good operation here, with good staff and a system that looks after itself.

Mick will have torn down the A34 this morning, making phone calls and swearing at drivers preventing his swift arrival at Lavington Stud. They'll not be making their way to work on a Monday morning in order to earn a living; they'll be there to prevent Mick from viewing a handful of yearlings in Sussex. Everyone is to blame, although that's the life we live in, I suppose. It's a world of either heroes or zeroes.

And Mick's not the only one to apportion blame or abuse. We had a winner last week in the form of King Crimson, an inconsistent sprint handicapper. He wins his fair share of races – five now – but he's as likely to win as he is to run a stinker. He won last Thursday at 25/1, beating several rivals who had trounced him on his previous racecourse appearance. The very fact that he was 25/1 was an indication of his form and record, but he's a front-runner with his own ideas as to how the world works, and Thursday, on soft ground at the tail of the season, he blazed a trail and was never sighted; an easy winner by nearly two lengths at Brighton under Charlie Bishop. Now, we often receive abusive emails, usually from punters who have backed a well-fancied favourite. They range in levels of abuse and rage: 'You're a fucking useless trainer, Channon. Why don't you fuck off and take up football again,' is a regular suggestion, while a few more sinister emails stick longer in the memory. I remember when an odds-on shot was beaten just after the accident. It was dreadful, but so outrageous, it didn't warrant much considera-tion: 'You fucking cunt. The worst thing you ever did was survive that car crash.'

These people *are* out there. The King Crimson abuse came from a different viewpoint, however. This was for actually winning a race with an outsider rather than losing one with a well-fancied runner:

From: Ajax69

Subject: Cheating

You fucking cheat, cheating trainers robbing punters of there [sic]
money from cheating the sooner you cheating trainers get hauled in
front of the stewards some of us punters would stand a chance but we
don't cheating trainers. cheats.

Ajax is not a member of the fan club.

It's a common theme, though. Conspiracy theories abound
in betting circles, with trainers seemingly at the forefront of a
wide-ranging and all encompassing conspiracy to rob the betting
fraternity of their money. There have been people found guilty
of corruption, of course, but I'll be buggered if Mick is a cheat.
Some of the rage-fuelled accusations make me weep with joy.
They give Mick way too much credit in terms of the underhand
means they accuse him of employing. I have this image of Mick
logging on to his Betfair account, on his iPhone, laying one of
our horses for thousands of pounds. This is a man who calls the
remote control for the telly 'the Machine'.

The best moments, however, are the punters who are just so
angry that they add the personal touch – and there's nothing
better than the written word. Emails amuse, but someone willing
to put pen to paper is a truly underrated and now all too rare
event. N. Conlon delivered just that a few years ago:

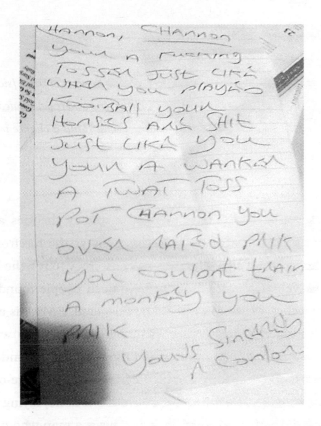

I don't think life gets any better than that. He doesn't express exactly what we can't train a monkey to do, and the 'Yours Sincerely' sign off is better than sublime. I love that letter.

WHO? WHAT? WHERE? WHAT?

WEDNESDAY 28 OCTOBER 2015

So we're in the office when in walks Brian O'Neil, the same Brian O'Neil of my childhood who built that stable block with Bobby Stokes while Mick was the foreman. Brian is unique. He's up here twice a week at least, and helps out around the place by washing cars, raking the driveway and putting Mick in a foul mood – mainly because Brian wakes Mick up when he arrives. That's usually at about five o'clock in the morning.

Brian's 70 now and today he's got a replica Saints shirt for Mick to sign for a sixtieth birthday present for a friend of Maureen's (it's not important who Maureen is but, rest assured, she's lovely). Mick, 66, tells Brian to hold it down so that the shirt doesn't crease and mess up the autograph that he's about to sign in thick black permanent marker. 'Who's it to, then?' he asks.

'What?' says Brian.

'Whose birthday is it?'

'I don't know.'

'What do you mean you don't know? You've just asked me to sign it for someone's birthday.'

'Yeah, but Maureen asked me to get it done.'

'She must have told you who it was for.'

'She did. But I forgot.'

'Fucking hell.'

Is it their time of life that makes such a relatively minor problem an unmitigated disaster? I thought of a brilliant solution: 'Is Maureen still on her old number, Brian? I'll call her and get the name and he can sign it later.'

'I don't know.'

'What do you mean you don't know?'

'I just pop round her house for a cup of tea. I don't have her number.'

'All right, I'll call Phil, then.'

Phil is 62 now, four years younger than his brother. He answers.

'Phil, is Maureen still on her old number?' I read the number out.

'No, she's moved house.'

'Well, have you got a mobile number for her?'

'Hang on a minute.' Bleeps and cursing were prevalent for quite some time. Phil struggles with his phone in the same way as his big brother. He eventually comes back to me, 'Maureen's number is 0 2 3 8 0 7 8—'

'That's her *old* number, Phil.'

'Oh yeah, I'll be buggered if I can use this bloody phone. I'll call you back.'

Mick was on the phone to Henrietta Knight talking about a hurdler he was trying to buy for Tim Radford. He's had a few in mind for quite some time now and was trying to detail what he thought would fit the bill to Hen after a conversation he'd had with a bloodstock agent called Tom Malone. While Mick's deep in conversation, Brian is standing there waving, asking me what Phil had to say about Maureen's friend's name. I'm trying to say that Phil doesn't know the name of Maureen's friend, that I was trying to speak to Maureen but we haven't got her number. Mick is waving Brian away because he's trying to deal with eight things at once. Brian's wondering why Phil might know the name of Maureen's friend, and then Phil rings back to say that he can't find Maureen's number, after all.

All I know is that Brian got half the job done, Phil can't work his phone, Mick doesn't care either way, and I ought to give up trying. As I left to see the yearlings I heard Mick saying, 'Anyway, I had a chat with that bloodstock agent, Tim Maloney . . .'

Who the fuck is Tim Maloney?

WATCHING ARCHIE

WEDNESDAY 4 NOVEMBER 2015

Alan Lee advised me to conclude this book at the end of the Flat season in November. It's now November, although the hope of ending it with a top-level success in the horseracing field has faded soon enough.

We've had a half-decent year with plenty of winners in its latter half, but I can't give you a rousing send-off, a climax of glory and success like a blockbuster movie. This is how things have turned out in our little world. I'm glad my dad's going to be OK, though. That's the main positive I'm taking out of 2015. I'll be honest; this book lark hasn't gone the way I thought it would at all.

When I started writing, after Cheltenham in the spring, it certainly wasn't supposed to be a catalogue of disasters, moaning, mishaps and meanderings about personal failures – as enjoyable as they've been. It was supposed to be something different. I'm not sure what, exactly, but certainly not this. It's been similar to the moment when, as a very small boy, I decided that I'd one day be the captain of Saints and score in front of Grandma Avril, sitting in her front row seat of the upper West Stand at the Dell. It never occurred to me that it wouldn't happen. Grandma Avril always assured me that it would. But hopes and dreams are a long way away from reality. My reality is good, though. I have great friends, and something of a dysfunctional but fine family. I'm grateful for that.

Therefore, I'll leave you with an afternoon spent at King George V sports ground in Winchester, right next to the M3, and the quarter-final of the southern pool of the national Under-13s Cup: Westgate School v Norman Gate School. Archie Morrall is playing wide right for the hosts, in front of his Grandad Mick, just as I did at Bakers Drove thirty years ago for Mansel Juniors before that bollocking in the passenger seat of his green Merc on the way home.

I drove there today. It was way too late for PopMaster so we avoided the awkward silences where important things could be said by listening to Radio 5 Live and talking about whether Mobsta should run in a Listed race at Doncaster on Saturday. 'Well, let's have a look in the morning. If he runs above himself and can only finish fifth, that'll fuck him for next season,' I said.

'Yeah, but, you know, he's a fucking racehorse.'

'Yeah, but there's not much point if he doesn't win and goes up in the weights.'

'I know, but you know, I'm keeping the fucker. Got bid a hundred and twenty grand for him this morning, but, you know, if I keep selling everything we've got that's any good, we'll be fucked for next year.'

I already know this, and I already know that he'll run on Saturday, regardless of my input. I worry about the future all too much – having horses that can compete, those that can keep Mick in touch with the big boys to satisfy his demands for competition, success and a reason to get up every day. I want him to be happy. Not satisfied – that's impossible – just happy will do.

For all that he's ever done with his life – Saints player, England player, Saints Cup winner, England captain, racehorse trainer, Group 1 winner, Royal Ascot winner; serial winner – here's me; I'm trying to help him.

I'm trying today as well. He's here watching his grandson run his socks off because his grandson wants him to be here. His grandson wants his grandad's attention. Nicky called me yesterday to ask if I could get him down to watch Archie, and I've managed it. That's how I measure success.

Nicky has never wanted Mick's attention because she received very little and is different to all of us. She'd like it, I'm sure, but she's never had it. She wants it for her kids, though. That's how blokes get away with murder, I reckon. A certain detachment makes you crave attention, and Mick inspires others to crave his.

Nicky's kids love their Grandad Mick. He's standing on the sidelines of a playing field just outside Winchester in his big jacket and flat cap. It's a blustery autumn afternoon and he looks on between the collar and peak, witnessing a thriller. Archie's Westgate take the lead halfway through the first half after missing a series of chances. Their centre-forward, Jack, passes up the opportunity to smash a cross first time with his right foot and chooses to swivel and hit it left-footed into the top corner instead. A great goal.

'Is he left-footed?' I ask his mum.

'Yes, he doesn't know what to do with the other one!' she says ecstatically.

'What a great goal!' says Mick – he genuinely meant it as well. We're all clapping and smiling: me, Mick, Nicky, Archie's dad Guy, and a handful of other proud parents. Mick looks happy. Archie is trying to act as though he's focused on the game, but I'm watching him and he's watching out for us watching him.

He's a wiry little lad, all rag and bone, very athletic, very bright but shy as well – a clever kid, hugely self-conscious, but intelligent; trying all the time. He exchanges passes and scampers after the return down the right wing in front of us.

'He's got a good brain on him!' Mick says with a smile of pride.

He's right as well. Archie's physically weak at the moment and muscled out of plenty of the game, but he knows exactly what he wants to do if only the body was able. He'll get stronger in time but, right now, there are bigger kids about him.

As the second half kicks off Archie is set free down the right and knocks in a near perfect cross that Jack just fails to get on the end of.

'That was the game there!' I say, as though I'm an authority on schoolboy football.

'I reckon you're right,' was Mick's reply.

True enough, Norman Gate took the game by the scruff of the neck as they got the equaliser, a second and then a third inside the next ten minutes. Archie and his Westgate teammates visibly crumbled with disappointment.

'The number four, the black lad in the middle and the little lad up front have just got that bit of class. That's what's done us,' was Mick's assessment.

'Plus we're kicking uphill this half,' I added.

'That hasn't helped either,' Mick accepted.

Full time: Westgate School 1–3 Norman Gate School. The kids were in bits. Proper disappointment. That's life right there.

Mick's phone rang.

'All right? Lesley? Yeah, where are we at?'

We have three horses going through the sales ring at Doncaster today and he wanders off to control the sales ring in south Yorkshire.

Archie doesn't want any conversational attention. He's 12 now and it's embarrassing to have your mum and dad there, let alone your uncle and grandad. He slopes off with his teammates, his school friends. I loved that bit. You could see that in the way they played. They're a good side, Westgate. Bright, intelligent and together.

Mick is 20 yards away, shouting at Lesley down the phone: 'Go to five grand! I'm not having my pants pulled down over that filly. She's worth at least fucking ten. That's what she's worth!'

In different ways Mick and I are bright, intelligent and together. I just can't work out how.

'This is where Terry Paine grew up. He played here as a kid,' I said, as we were driving out of the King George V playing fields. I thought Mick would want something to talk about other than work. Terry Paine was his hero.

'Did he?'

'Yeah.'

He was somewhere else. 'We got eleven grand for Popeswood. That's probably the market, I suppose. He's rated eighty-two, though. You'd have thought he'd be worth more than that.'

'Yeah.'

'Good game, though, wasn't it? I really enjoyed that,' he said.

'It was, mate. Archie tries, he's bright and knows what he's about.'

'Fucking hell he tries! He's just so weak, though. He's got a great attitude but he needs to strengthen up! He's like that fucking Paddy Pilley.'

'Yeah,' I laughed inside. Silly old fucker. Never switches off. I thought back to the bollocking in the green Merc. 'Great game. Took me back to when I was that age. Games like that were the only things that ever mattered. Do you remember the Sunday mornings when you used to watch me with Brian and Stokesy?'

He nodded and thought back. 'That was different, though.'

'How?'

'You just played. They are all intelligent now, those kids. They pass it and play properly. You just played.'

'Back in the day, eh?' I was laughing.

'Yeah! The last generation before computers fucked everyone up.'

'I remember a sliding tackle I made in the last minute at Bakers Drove. I was covered in mud and Brian went mental, thought it was great. I remember Bobby standing there with a fag, and you laughing.'

Mick thought for a bit. I knew he had no recollection of the tackle. 'How long has Bob been gone?'

'Believe it or not, he was only four years older than I am now.'

'Fucking hell. How old are you?'

'Forty.'

'How long ago was that, then?'

'Nineteen ninety-five, the year I broke my neck.'

'Yeah, but Bob – he'll never be old, will he? *Stokesy!*' He let out a laugh laced with affection.

We drove home to get ready for tomorrow.

We're going to be all right. That's what I think, anyway. For all of the bickering and disagreements, for all of his grumpy dissatisfaction with more or less everything, at least I have my old man. The rest of it will look after itself because, as long as he's around things will get done, horses will be fit and we'll get up and do the same thing tomorrow, whether we win, lose or draw. That's all he wants to do: get up, graft away and try to win.

I'm asked the same question everywhere I go by whoever I meet: 'How's your dad?'

It's been a tricky one to answer in the second half of this year but, if I look back and try to nail it down, I'd say this: 'He's hard-working, barking mad, sometimes insufferable but, ulti-mately, he's just incredible.'

I love my dad.

(Don't tell him, though. That would be showing weakness.)

EPILOGUE 1 – 'I'VE WRITTEN A BOOK'

THURSDAY 7 APRIL 2016

I got back from five days in Gran Canaria yesterday. It rained every day.

Not a complete disaster because it meant that I could pull this book together in the apartment I'd taken.

Today I'd decided to tell Mick about the book. He had no idea that I'd been writing it.

I was going to tell him before first lot but it was difficult to get his attention. At six o'clock this morning he was reading the birthday section of the *Racing Post*:

'Would you say I'm older than Luca Cumani?' he asked. 'Yes,' I replied. 'Fuck off! I'm not having that. Fuck me, no way! Fucking Luca Cumani, younger than me? Bollocks.'

I bottled it for a couple of hours but eventually blurted it out as third lot were walking home. 'I finished a book on holiday.' I hadn't fully committed to it.

'You read plenty of books, don't you?'

I had to just go for it.

'No, Dad – I finished *writing* a book.'

'You what?'

'I've written a book.'

'What about?'

'About last year and everything around it.'

'Really? Am I in it?'

'Yeah. You're in a lot of it. I need you to read it.'

'Why do you want me to read it? I'll read it when it comes out.'

'Thing is, I need your approval. Everything from last year is in it. There's stuff about your health, and I don't want to upset you. The way I see it . . . if you don't like it, I can just keep it for the family, as a sort of archive for the kids: Archie, Milo and Evie and their kids, if nothing else. If you don't want it public then that's fine. I just wanted to do it, and it helped me. That's all.' I was red in the face and shaking.

I'd argue that this was the hardest thing I've ever done.

'Well, I'd better read it then, hadn't I?'

EPILOGUE 2 – 'I'VE READ YOUR BOOK'

THURSDAY 28 APRIL, 2016

Obviously it happened at the most inappropriate moment – when the horses were walking past us and we were pairing them up for morning exercise.

'You join Harrison, Keith; and you join October Storm, Steve! Jon, you lead and Paul will put Czabo in the middle . . .' and then he just came out with, 'I've read your book. It's good, all fine, but I just think you ought to get someone else to read it because I'm thick as shit . . . Lenka! You join Epsom Icon and go steady, we don't need any more fuck-ups this morning!'

We got in the wagon and I knew he didn't want to talk about it in any real detail. By squeezing his approval in between organising the horses, he thought he'd manage to reduce the personal nature of the subject to the bare minimum. But I had to make sure he knew what I'd asked of him.

'I wasn't asking you to review it, Mick. I was asking you if it was acceptable, because there's a lot in there regarding your health and that.' He didn't listen. I think he missed the whole point.

'Can you not get in a bit about Hugh Bowman? That always makes me laugh when you talk about him and his missus that night in the pub.'

'Dad, everything in the book is there for a reason. It's not just about chucking in random anecdotes about an Australian jockey and his wife having a row.'

'Fine. That's fine, but that *is* a funny story. You should get someone other than me to read it.'

'I *have*. Brough Scott and all my friends have read it. The ones I mentioned in the foreword.'

'That's fine, then. I don't give a shit about what you've said about me. I've got enough to say about everyone else, haven't I?'

So there you go.

Approval.

Of a sort.

CAST OF CHARACTERS

In order of appearance:

Alan Ball

My dad's best friend: footballer, raconteur and friend to everyone. During the Ashes cricket series in Australia during the winter of 2006–2007 I was his bookies runner. There was a horse called The Butler, a sprinter whom we backed every week. We all loved The Butler as much as we loved 'Bally'.

Phil Channon

My dad's brother, my uncle. A true family man and one-time talented athlete. Now the proprietor of Hylands fruit and veg store in Bishop's Waltham in Hampshire. I do a lot of shoplifting at Hylands. It makes sense, economically.

Mick Channon

My dad and the hero of this tale. Southampton Football Club's record goalscorer, England international with 21 goals in 46 appearances, a winner of the FA Cup and Milk Cup, and now a successful racehorse trainer based at West Ilsley in Berkshire. I'm his assistant. They say never work with children or animals, but he works with both. I'd like to add to that adage: you should never work with children, animals or your parents. Thankfully he received the all clear in May 2016.

Somersby

A racehorse. Frustrating, talented, slightly neurotic. A bit like a racehorse trainer.

Bobby Stokes

My dad grew up with him at Southampton Football Club. Scorer of the club's most important goal in the 1976 FA Cup final. A kinder man you couldn't meet. He died too young, in 1995. My hero.

Jane Channon

My mum. Hard working, long suffering, very kind and lovely. Well, she is my mum.

Needless Shouting

Another horse. Half decent, genuine, honest, fun and owned by a syndicate. Quite grumpy. Loved his food. 'Feed me and fuck off!' was his mantra. He's since moved to North Yorkshire. He's still in racing.

Daniel Cremin

An apprentice jockey. Funny, hard working but needed an arm round him. Received a bollocking every other day when having a good week. Now in Sydney Australia. His Snapchat updates are quite hilarious.

Kevin Keegan

A former footballer with England, Liverpool and Southampton among others. Also a manager of England and Manchester City. A good man, unless cornered by a journalist live on television after a disappointing defeat for Manchester City on a Sunday afternoon at Preston North End.

Bossy Guest
A talented, slightly flawed three-year-old racehorse. He was a shining light of the 2015 Flat season – to a point. A colt who became the source of admiration and heartache. Things haven't gone right for Bossy in 2016 but he remains with us at West Ilsley with the hope that he'll return to form.

Malabar
Another talented three-year-old racehorse. The provider of the highpoint of 2015 at Glorious Goodwood.

Jill Channon
My dad's wife, my stepmother. We've been through a lot together, most memorably the Accident & Emergency doors of the Nottingham University Hospital.

Tim Corby
One of my dad's best friends. He was his right-hand man, a worrier, a carer and an ally. An enthusiast for life. Tragically, he died in a car crash while driving my dad and brother home from Doncaster yearling sales in August 2008.

Jack Channon
My half-brother. A good lad. Horseracing mad and lucky to be here. I'm glad he is.

Uncle John
Technically my great uncle, Mick and Phil Channon's genuine uncle. Younger brother to 'the Boss', Grandma Channon. John is barking mad.

Grandma

Mick and Phil's mum, the greatest woman in the world, lives at West Ilsley Stables.

Charlie Bishop

A talented former apprentice jockey with my dad and now a fully-fledged professional at the stable yard. A constant source of blame.

Paddy Pilley

The youngest apprentice jockey and the biggest source of frustration to his trainer. Very talented but a bit dopey. He was a homegrown product, so bollockings were expected and accepted like the weather. He's since moved on and will be riding out in Australia in the winter.

Mick Quinn

Former footballer and teammate of my dad, now a racehorse trainer and radio presenter. I opted to stay with him when I had a month's trial at Coventry City Football Club as an 18-year-old. Not the best landlord for an aspiring footballer to stay with.

Matt Le Tissier

Former footballer with Southampton, and a hero of the city. Brilliant at most things, including penalties, free-kicks and phone calls to victims of spinal injuries on matchdays.

Nicky Channon

My sister. Pretty much perfect. Great mum, great daughter, great friend to many. Utterly dependable. This has annoyed me throughout my life.

Marc Middlemiss

The opposite of my sister. A shambles but a valued friend with a sometimes financially suicidal approach to gambling. A Geordie with a great eye for fun, though. Now and then a flutter has paid dividends.

Neil Channon

Phil Channon's son, my cousin. Assistant to his dad (tragic soul) at Hylands fruit and veg store in Bishop's Waltham in Hampshire. Owner of two sheds.

Peter Taplin

My dad's longest-serving owner. A farmer, a friend and an all round good man.

Sue Bunney

Newer to racehorse ownership than Peter but just as solid a person. Southampton supporter and somebody who I need for a little bit of sanity.

Gandvik

Gandvik was a racehorse. He now lives in a field. The hardiest racehorse ever, who had to be retired. Quite simply, he didn't know when he was going to snap in half. We had to stop him before he did something stupid. A source of immense admiration and respect. Blatantly stupid. Entering retraining in 2017. Whatever he ends up doing he'll give it 100 per cent.

John Marston

Sportsman, competitor and my golfing nemesis. Also the catalyst for this book. Unfortunately, it was his death that started me off. I miss him.

Brian O'Neil

Another of my dad's teammates from Southampton. Very talented and incredibly loyal. Mad as a hatter, Dad's most loyal ally and a regular visitor to the stables. I ought to reiterate that he's as mad as a hatter.

Grandad Jack

Mick and Phil's dad, my grandad. Wore paisley ties and green cardigans for the entire length of the time that I knew him. Also specialised in wearing trousers somewhere near his nipple line, with a zip that must have measured over a foot in length. Much loved, much missed.

Undoubtedly his position as the consort of one of England's 'queens of crime' made Edmund Walker-Pyne's archaeological excavations in Egypt more newsworthy than usual, especially as it was hinted loudly that they were being funded by the British and American reading public and were no more than an expensive hobby for the dashing Edmund – a hobby which kept him well out of range of the army of young female (pointedly younger than his wife) fans who had come to swoon over the adventures of his fictional alter ego Rex Troughton.

All thinly veiled sniping ceased abruptly on the outbreak of war when it became publicly known that Edmund, a keen sailor in his youth and a member of the Royal Navy Volunteer Reserve, had abandoned the desert to serve his country on the high seas. Archaeology's loss was likely to become popular fiction's gain, as Rex Troughton, it was assumed, would now put his considerable skills as an amateur sleuth to fighting the biggest villain he had yet encountered within a dust jacket.

There was genuine sympathy for Evadne Childe when the news was released that she had lost both her husband and her muse, as Edmund achieved the unenviable distinction of being among the first British fatalities with the war not yet six weeks old. Given the rank of sub-lieutenant, Edmund had been assigned as a signals and communications officer on the passenger steamer SS *West Riding*, bound for Rangoon, which was a hundred miles off Cape Finisterre when it was shelled and sunk by a surfaced U-boat with the loss of more than sixty passengers and crew. It was little consolation to his widow to learn that Edmund had done his duty and his radio distress calls had been heard by an American steamship which was quickly able to pick up survivors, but not quickly enough to prevent Sub-Lieutenant Walker-Pyne from dying of his injuries in a leaky lifeboat. His body, and the survivors, were unloaded at Bordeaux, and a British consulate official (and avid reader of detective fiction) arranged for interment in the Protestant cemetery there, writing personally to express his sympathies to Evadne Childe, care of her publisher, and offering to assist in arranging a visit to her husband's grave. It was an offer Evadne politely refused, pointing out that there was a war on, and her journey would not, technically, be necessary as long as the consulate could supply her with a plan of the cemetery and the exact geographical co-ordinates of Edmund's

Please forgive me, say you forgive me. You won't tell Gilpin's, will you?'

The girl was contrite and her embarrassment genuine and Evadne Childe had no intention of tormenting her; the fact that she was concerned about her faux pas being reported to her employers, who she knew valued Evadne's services more than hers, merely emphasized her youth. Outwardly worldly and confident, mentally she was an innocent in the school playground. What could she know about widowhood?

'No, I will not tell Gilpin's.' Evadne hoped the girl did not notice the twinkle in her eye. 'My dear child, it would surely be pointless for a mere vicar's daughter to try and tell a publisher anything about being rude and tactless to an author?'

Seven years and seven successful novels had left Evadne Childe in a position of armed neutrality with her publishing house, the firm of J.P. Gilpin and Company of New York and London; a position in which many an author who has tasted early success find themselves.

It had been Gilpin's, or JP's, as they were sometimes known, who had picked up Evadne's first detective novel, *A Richer Dust*, for publication initially in America and then in Britain, in 1933. The book had enjoyed more than modest sales and immoderately generous reviews, with Charles Williams, writing in the *Westminster Gazette*, calling it 'a singularly agreeable book' and no less than Dorothy Sayers hailing it as a 'bloodthirsty yet highly moral debut' in the *Sunday Times*. Seven more novels had followed, all with increasing sales and all featuring her detective hero, the resourceful and breathtakingly handsome Rex Troughton, and many who knew her had said it was fate, though Evadne favoured mere chance, that having created a dashing hero on the page who was an amateur sleuth but professional archaeologist, she should then fall in love in life (as well as on the page) with a real archaeologist, Edmund Walker-Pyne.

In those pages of the popular press which tottered on the knife edge between 'arts and culture' and 'society gossip', the marriage of a successful female writer of detective stories at the age of forty-seven to a penniless archaeologist, albeit a Cambridge one, some twenty-two years her junior, filled many column inches in that brief period of calm between the Abdication Crisis in England and the rather more significant crisis looming in Europe.

Evadne Walker-Pyne, better known to the reading public by her maiden name of Evadne Childe, smoothed her napkin back across the lap of her skirt and tried to suppress a smile.

'My dear Veronica, I am, I believe, a highly valued asset to the publishing house which, out of charity I presume, sees fit to employ you. Your duties today consist of buying me lunch and flattering me ceaselessly; if, that is, you want to take possession of your firm's next bestselling detective story. Do not attempt to shock me with outrageous tales of the sordid goings-on in those dim and dusty clubs you frequent down Dean Street. I am a respectable, middle-aged English woman who earns her own living by writing modestly successful stories of murder and mayhem, and I have visited Egypt on more than one occasion. I am, therefore, unshockable. Though as a writer, of course, I am – purely professionally, you understand – always interested in the less respectable establishments you frequent. I rely on you for my research into the twilight world of the capital's clubland.'

Veronica Hatherall crushed out her cigarette into a small metal ashtray and sighed loudly; the sort of sigh practised to perfection by young women with very little to actually sigh about.

'I could shock you if I wanted to,' she said, producing a small lacquered mirror and lipstick from her purse, 'with tales of the clubs I visited last year in New York. There were some, off Forty-Second Street, which shocked even me. They're so much more *strict* than the ones down Dean Street, if I can put it that way. Really quite aggressively strict, if you know what I mean.'

Veronica concentrated on repairing her lipstick, airily ignoring her guest, but when the older woman failed to rise to the bait she snapped shut her compact.

'Oh, don't look at me like that! This Bore War is, well, boring. A girl has to find her thrills somewhere.'

'The war is no longer boring, you foolish little thing! You might think the real shooting war has only just started, but for those on our ships out there on the sea, it began months ago and it was far from boring.'

Evadne Childe spoke quietly and deliberately, but each word carried a weight and force of a pile-driving hammer and Veronica Hatherall recoiled under the impact.

'Oh my God, Evie, I am so sorry. I simply wasn't thinking.

ONE
Shooting Gallery

'But that must have been an absolute hoot, my dear! I mean to say, Evadne Childe, positively the *queen* of detective-story writers, having to ask the bumbling British policeman for advice on a murder weapon! Surely, it ought to be the other way round, shouldn't it?'

'If you can't behave yourself, Veronica, at least keep your voice down. It's too early to be decently drunk and I have a lot to say to you, so pay attention.'

'Yes, miss.'

'And don't give me *that* look, young lady. You know it doesn't work on me, and anyway, you have shreds of tobacco in your lipstick, which make you look quite common. No, bottom lip. Oh, come here, I'll do it. Spit.'

Had anyone been observing them closely (though no one was), they would have assumed they were witnessing a simple domestic scene and could have been forgiven for thinking this was standard mother-hen behaviour as the older woman held up her napkin for the younger one to wet, daintily, with spittle for a minor, but necessary, cleaning operation.

The two women were lunching together at a table dangerously close (had they considered it) to the cross-taped glass window bearing the legend *Café Bucci* which looked out on to Charlotte Street. They were not, however, mother and daughter, but author and 'publisher's representative' respectively and, even though the latter, and younger, of the two was the one having to have her face wiped in public, it would be she who would pay the bill.

'What do you mean by *that look*?' asked Veronica huskily, fluttering her eyelashes at the older woman. 'If you mean my own patented "petulant schoolgirl" look – well, it might not work on you, but it has never failed me when I needed it to persuade a well-filled uniform to buy me a drink or get me into a nightclub. Oh, I'm sorry, Evie, have I shocked you?'

(vii) Write to Reuben telling him to have car meet me. Ask if Miss Kitto is still in business.

(viii) Collect laundry. Buy coffee to take to Essex as Mother will not have any. (Also whisky and gin just in case!)

(ix) Have lunch with Veronica to deliver (final?) manuscript.

(x) Buy gun oil and clean Daddy's service revolver. Ask at police station where to buy ammunition.

PART ONE
Evadne Child, 1940

Extract from the journals (unpublished) of Evadne Walker-Pyne (née Childe).

We are alone. The capitulation of the French was accepted with a strange calm. There was more fear (and a touch of panic) at the news of the surrender of poor little Belgium in May, but now the inevitability of it all spreads across the country like a blanket of autumn fog barging aside what looks like being a summer of glorious weather.

For the last nine months we have been in a sinister trance. This 'Bore War' has put us all to sleep, although as children have been conceived and born in the time we have been at war, clearly not everyone was bored. And then, whilst we were rubbing the crust from our eyes, our friends and allies disappeared one by one: Denmark, Norway, Holland, Belgium, now France.

With Edmund gone, I am more alone than most and, if I cannot have my husband at my side, I will not stay in London. I don't care what the authorities say about whether my journey is neces-sary or not. I deem it is. I have a mother to care for, after all, so I will de-camp to wildest Essex even if I end up having to walk there.

Note to Self: Things to do

    (i)   *Deposit leases, jewellery, Will, so forth, at bank.*
   (ii)   *Warn House Manager about empty flat – see to gas, electric, etc.*
  (iii)   *Dispose of house plants and put out rubbish, cancel milk.*
  (iv)   *Give forwarding address to postman.*
   (v)   *Stop newspapers. Tip newspaper lad.*
  (vi)   *Leave cash for cleaner with doorman. £5 or £10?*

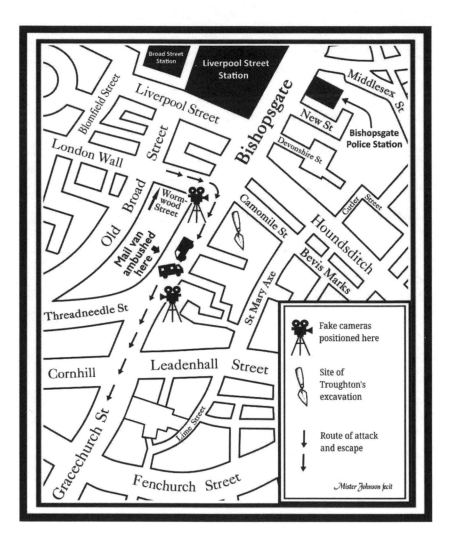

Frontispiece to *Camera Obscuring*
(a Rex Troughton adventure)
by Evadne Childe
J. Gilpin & Co., London and New York
1952

Part Five: Albert Campion, 1965

CONTENTS

Also by Evadne Childe

A Richer Dust (1933)
Death in the Diplomatic Bag (1934)
Murder on Air (1935)
Here Be Dragons (1936)
Tears of a Clown (1936)
Right Body, Wrong Grave (1937)
The Beauregard Inheritance (1938)
The Murders at Six Mile Bottom (1939)
With Smoke and Mirrors (1941)
The Body in the Blitz (1943)
Dark Moon Over Soho (1945)
The Bottle Party Murders (1946)
Old Bones, New Bones (1947)
The Coffin Comes Free (1948)
Burial Mound (1949)
The Moving Mosaic (1950)
The Robbers Are Coming to Town (1951)
Camera Obscuring (1952)
Murder Imperial (1955)
The Collector of Skulls (1958)
Terrifying Angel (1960)
Pearls Before Swine (1963)
Cozenage (1966)*

*Published posthumously

In his long fictional career (1929–68) at the hands of his creator Margery Allingham, Mr Albert Campion was never a policeman, simply a very gifted amateur detective. He did, however, work closely with a triptych of notable policemen: Superintendent Stanislaus Oates, Detective Chief Inspector P. 'Freddie' Yeo and Detective Inspector Charles Luke. All three rose to the very top of their profession over the years and remained, remarkably, on very good terms with Mr Campion.

Readers familiar with Margery Allingham's backlist and keen to explore that of Evadne Childe may notice that *The Robbers Are Coming to Town* was the provisional title of Allingham's classic, *The Tiger in the Smoke*, and *Pearls Before Swine* was the title adopted in 1945 for the American edition of *Coroner's Pidgin*. For the uninitiated, the Allingham novels are well worth seeking out. Evadne Childe's much less accomplished work is rather more difficult to find.

This first world edition published 2020
in Great Britain and the USA by
SEVERN HOUSE PUBLISHERS LTD of
Eardley House, 4 Uxbridge Street, London W8 7SY.
Trade paperback edition first published
in Great Britain and the USA 2021 by
SEVERN HOUSE PUBLISHERS LTD.

British Library Cataloguing in Publication Data
A CIP catalogue record for this title is available from the British Library.

ISBN-13: 978-0-7278-8961-4 (cased)
ISBN-13: 978-1-78029-710-1 (trade paper)
ISBN-13: 978-1-4483-0431-8 (e-book)

This is a work of fiction. Names, characters, places and incidents
are either the product of the author's imagination or are used fictitiously.
Except where actual historical events and characters are being described
for the storyline of this novel, all situations in this publication are
fictitious and any resemblance to actual persons, living or dead,
business establishments, events or locales is purely coincidental.

All Severn House titles are printed on acid-free paper.

Severn House Publishers support the Forest Stewardship Council™ [FSC™],
the leading international forest certification organisation.
All our titles that are printed on FSC certified paper carry the FSC logo.

MR CAMPION'S SÉANCE

Mike Ripley

Also by Mike Ripley

Margery Allingham's Albert Campion

MR CAMPION'S FAREWELL *
MR CAMPION'S FOX *
MR CAMPION'S FAULT *
MR CAMPION'S ABDICATION *
MR CAMPION'S WAR *
MR CAMPION'S VISIT *

The Fitzroy Maclean Angel series

LIGHTS, CAMERA, ANGEL
ANGEL UNDERGROUND
ANGEL ON THE INSIDE
ANGEL IN THE HOUSE
ANGEL'S SHARE
ANGELS UNAWARE
Etc.

Other titles

DOUBLE TAKE
BOUDICA AND THE LOST ROMAN
THE LEGEND OF HEREWARD *

Non-fiction

SURVIVING A STROKE
KISS KISS, BANG BANG

* *available from Severn House*

MR CAMPION'S SÉANCE